Bearing the Bad News

Contemporary
American
Literature and
Culture

BEARING THE BAD NEWS

By Sanford Pinsker

University of Iowa Press 🌵 Iowa City

University of Iowa Press, Iowa City 52242
Copyright © 1990 by the University of Iowa
All rights reserved
Printed in the United States of America
First edition, 1990

Printed on acid-free paper

Library of Congress Cataloging-in-Publication Data

Pinsker, Sanford.
Bearing the bad news: contemporary American literature and
culture/by Sanford Pinsker. — 1st ed.
p. cm.
ISBN 0-87745-292-X (alk. paper)
1. American literature—20th century—History and criticism.
2. Literature and society—United States—History—20th century.
3. United States—Civilization—1970–   4. Social problems in
literature.   I. Title.
PS225.P56   1990   90-35570
810.9′005—dc20   CIP

for Stan Lindberg,

who prodded me to write,

and then to rewrite

Contents

Acknowledgments

The following essays have appeared in these publications in a slightly different form: "Philip Rahv's 'Paleface and Redskin' – Fifty Years Later," "*The Catcher in the Rye* and All: Is the Age of Formative Books Over?" "Comedy and Cultural Timing: The Lessons of Robert Benchley and Woody Allen" in the *Georgia Review*; "Lenny Bruce: *Shpritzing* the *Goyim*/Shocking the Jews" in Sarah Blacher Cohen, ed., *Jewish Wry* (1986); "Bashing the Liberals: How the Neoconservatives Make Their Point," "Modernist Culture, the Cunning of History, and Paul de Man," and "Lost Causes/ Marginal Hopes: The Collected Elegies of Irving Howe" in *Virginia Quarterly Review*; "Gestures of Indefinite Revolt: College Life through Fictional Prisms" in the *Colorado Review*; "Saul Bellow and the Special Comedy of Urban Life" in *Ontario Review*; and "Revisionist Thought, Academic Power, and the Aging American Intellectual" in the *Gettysburg Review*.

Although this collection focuses on the varieties of bad news that permeate our culture, such essays generally are not written unless one is lucky enough to teach at a place that encourages, and supports, such writing, and where colleagues and students present countless opportunities to test out one's ideas and, more important perhaps, to have those ideas taken seriously. Lest there be any confusion, I am the "one" I have just written about, and an acknowledgments page strikes me as the proper place to announce this "good news."

Preface

To impose an arrangement onto a group of disparate essays is a bit like dragging Flem Snopes, William Faulkner's consummate wheeler-dealer, into court. You can subpoena his testimony – you can even make him act respectable – but as Mrs. Tull discovers, you're not likely to get much real satisfaction. It's much the same thing with journal articles that seek a more permanent place in the library stacks. One wants to believe that they belong between hard covers (indeed, that is the point introductions generally argue), but one also has the sinking feeling that this is precisely the sort of stunt Flem would pull if he were a professor.

Remember, too, that Faulkner's *The Hamlet* ends on a note as funny as it is ominously prophetic. After patiently trying to untangle Flem's complicated, wildly comic affairs, the Judge throws up his hands and admits publicly that he "can't stand it no more! This court's adjourned!" It's a delicious moment, but one destined for a long, and ultimately exasperating, run in American culture. For even as we celebrate Faulkner's updating of an Old Southwestern comic spirit that lies beyond law-and-order's grip, we recognize that the small claims court and civil suit are rapidly becoming for our world what the prison and the graveyard were for Hawthorne's. Public shame presumably mattered when Hester Prynne was paraded before the Salem citizenry sporting her Scarlet A; now one defines America as a land where, at any given moment, half the population is hard at work shamelessly filing a lawsuit against the other half.

I belabor this point because in our litigious times one does what one can to avoid trouble. So, I begin with what poets in the 1960s used to call a "confession," but which now travels under the legalese of "disclaimer." Unlike most solid citizens in the collected essays genre, mine comes into the world of letters waving its title, but not a title essay. Instead, I have used the notion of "bearing the bad news" as a general statement about what I take to be the curious position of literary criticism today.

Moreover, I have used the term in at least several senses – not only to point out that critics are often called upon to be messengers of bad news, that here a work of art misses the mark or there exceeds it, that the emperor who thinks he's draped in finery is naked or the author who has a fistful of honors is, in truth, overpraised, but also as a way of suggesting that serious literature helps critics to endure, to *bear*, the glitz-and-shlock our popular culture hurls at us.

What concerns me is less that readers will agree with my judgments on specific issues – an unlikely prospect at best – but, rather, that we will once again see this tension between what critics knock and what critics need as a matter of wider cultural import. As things stand now, the safest thing one could say about American culture is that we're going through something of a bad patch. Never has so much been written by so many about so little.

That said, however, let me hasten to add that my sense of the "bad news" is not so much that we have minimalists where once there were giants, or that critical theory is more comfortable talking about texts than about novels, stories, and poems. Rather, what we are stuck with is a condition in search of what T. S. Eliot called an objective correlative. His demonstration that the modern world is a "waste land" was a brilliant stroke; and while I would admit that our age has not been blessed, or cursed, with a similarly insightful tag, I am not yet willing to turn the problem over to Tom Wolfe (who coined the phrase "Me Decade") or to those pundits who raised the ante with what they called the "Brie" Generation.

My hope, of course, is that the essays I've selected will sharpen debate without generating still finer gradations of bad news, although I am aware that "producing" is yet another of the puns that collects around my title. Most of all, though, I hope that my essays do not behave *too* well in the court of public opinion. In some cases, I've straightened their ties, buffed their shoes, or made them spit out their chewing gum, but I think Flem would want me to let 'em rip. After all, many of them celebrate that sense of humor which, as other essays point out, we probably need more now than ever before.

BEARING THE BAD NEWS

Literary Culture, the Way It Was

The fiftieth anniversary of Philip Rahv's justly famous, enormously influential article "Paleface and Redskin" struck me as an occasion to reflect on the literary scene as Rahv saw it in 1939 as well as on the ways his schema of deeply divided temperaments might be extended, modified, or overturned in our own time.

Looking back – both at the way that a New York intellectual such as Rahv talked about literary culture during the heyday of journals such as the *Kenyon* or *Partisan Review* and at the ways that such discussions are conducted currently – I began to realize that the piece might serve as a general introduction, an overview, if you will – to the concerns I hope to raise in this collection. At issue is not only what we read, but also *how* and *why* we read as we do.

When my piece appeared in the *Georgia Review* I received a letter from a young graduate student who readily granted that American literature "can be read as a reflection of this country's diversity, or can be deconstructed to show that it serves that purpose," but who then went on to voice his reservations about such currently fashionable pursuits: "But if all we are doing to literature is reading it for historical purposes or deconstructing its languages and purposes to achieve marginal meanings, then we are in dire circumstances." Much as I enjoy letters from readers who tell me that I've hit the cultural nail on the head, I'm not sure I agree that our present condition is either as dire or as hopeless as he suggests. Indeed, there are times when I would prefer to argue that we live in what an old Chinese curse calls "interesting times" – fully realizing that one's person's curse is another's opportunity and somebody else's blessing. Nonetheless, I take some measure of comfort in knowing that there may well be a generation of graduate students out there who have grown disenchanted with efforts to separate literature from life, authors from novels, and culture itself from the life of the mind.

The second article in this section continues this discussion but pins it to my recollections of reading – and later, teaching – J. D. Salinger's *The Catcher in the Rye* and what this implies about the larger, more important matter of formative books per se. No doubt certain notes of nostalgia creep in, and perhaps a few notes of sadness as well, because it is hard to imagine a world in which books matter deeply to the young and harder still to think about what might pass as formative reading for a generation reared on "Sesame Street" and MTV.

The question, of course, is not whether a high school student has "gone through" Shakespeare or Milton, Austen or Hardy, but whether these authors have gone through the student. To be sure, others have been much concerned about the shape that required reading ought to take; I worry more about the disappearance of *un*required reading. For if students encounter literature only in the classroom they are not likely to know, much less to bring with them, the excitement and the passion that genuine reading requires.

The following section, then, sets the stage for my assessment of how contemporary American literature and contemporary American culture are inextricably related. "Bearing the bad news" properly begins these considerations.

Philip Rahv's "Paleface and Redskin" – Fifty Years Later

![decorative ornament]

That Philip Rahv's influential essay "Paleface and Redskin" first appeared in the pages of the *Kenyon Review* fifty years ago ought to give us pause – has it been *that* long? – as well as an opportunity for reflection (perhaps even for a symposium of the sort that *Partisan Review* loved to concoct, and that academic institutions then learned how to turn into three-day extravaganzas). But I suspect this is one literary anniversary that will pass without a modicum of fanfare. Where, after all, would one begin? By explaining who Philip Rahv was, and what the old, great days of the *Kenyon* and *Partisan* were like? By making a case for the literary essay when it has fallen on hard times? By reminding those who keep up with the latest theoretical news from France, the latest magical realists from South America, and the latest dissidents from Eastern Europe that the condition and the fate of *American* literature still matter?

Granted, much has changed since Rahv unloaded his thesis about the split personality in our most representative writers. As "Paleface and Redskin" would have it, American literature falls into two neatly packaged, diametrically opposed packages: either the "open-air poems of Walt Whitman" or the "drawing-room fictions of Henry James." Across this Great Divide each camp hurled its disapprovals, be they by way of raspberries and barbaric yawps or in the mannered cadences of a consciousness so finely wrought that life's messiness dared not intrude. It was an essay so eye-catching, so wonderfully schematic, so eminently usable that whole paragraphs were trotted out – usually unacknowledged – in hundreds of lecture halls and on not a few final examinations. No matter that Rahv took some pains to reckon the assets and liabilities that fastened to each position; no matter that Rahv was more interested in raising questions than he was in providing a quick litmus test for everyone from Anne Bradstreet to Ernest Hemingway. For better or worse, the words "paleface" and "redskin" stuck, and that is a fact of some consequence as one gives the essay a long retrospective look.

Admittedly, even Rahv's detractors would not hold him culpable for the oversimplifications, much less the misreadings, that have clustered around his essay. He set out to see American literature steady and whole, to provide the sort of overview that is conspicuously absent in contemporary treatments of our literature. But it is also true that Rahv's metaphors invite the oversimplifications that have dogged his essay's heels. Even its title – no doubt meant to be attention-grabbing at the time – can only strike us as problematic now. In short, given the essay's importance in the history of American literary criticism, what are we to do about the energies (e.g., of Blacks, women, *real* AmerIndians) and tensions that his schema conveniently leaves out?

Let me approach this problem by suggesting that there are rough parallels between Rahv's purpose and the combination of manifesto and prophecy that energized Emerson's 1844 essay "The Poet." In both cases, what mattered centrally was less the literature that preceded their respective moments than the cultural atmosphere they hoped to call into being. At its best, of course, literary criticism is a combination of assessment and injunction, but it is also true that the most memorable and significant literary essays find a way to fold the former into the pressing concerns of the latter. That is precisely the case in Emerson's essay, a piece that sets out to define *the* poet, the representative man who "stands among partial men for the complete man, and apprises us not of his wealth, but of the commonwealth." One hardly need belabor the case that Emerson had himself in mind – indeed, that everything in his public discourse from *Nature* (1836) onward argues for the poet as self-creating and self-justifying, as the perfect embodiment of what Quentin Anderson identifies as the Imperial Self:

> The poet is the sayer, the namer, and represents beauty. He is a sovereign, and stands on the centre. For the world is not painted, or adorned, but is from the beginning beautiful; and God has not made some beautiful things, but Beauty is the creator of the universe. Therefore the poet is not any permissive potentate, but is emperor in his own right.

That scholars and creative writers have subsequently appropriated the essay either to justify work already done (e.g., Poe's "The Philosophy of Composition") or to clarify the direction of their own work-in-progress is hardly surprising. For Emerson, the name of the American bard he imagined may have been Adam, patron saint of namers, but his *secret* name – his pseudonym, if you will – was Waldo. *He* is the one who would "announce that which no man foretold," *he* who would become "an utterer of the necessary and the casual."

But as Emerson discovered a decade later, the poet he described so lovingly by looking into his own transcendental heart turned out to be another sort altogether: "Walt Whitman, a kosmos, of Manhattan the son." In this sense, Rahv had better luck because he argued neither as poet nor as fictionist, neither as paleface nor as redskin. Instead, he wrote as one who believed that we read American literature to better read ourselves as Americans, and it is this spirit – rather than his specific observations about, say, Whitman or James – that gives his essay a contemporary significance. Moreover, the same Rahv who described the fundamental tension of American literature as pitting paleface against redskin also worried about its limitations. By 1939, Rahv was convinced that the battle was largely over, and that the redskins had won. They controlled the "main highway of literature" (i.e., the novel) and – in words that sounded for all the world like echoes of D. H. Lawrence's *Studies in Classic American Literature* (1923) – Rahv set about to ponder how much of this victory deserved the adjective "Pyrrhic":

The redskin writer in America is a purely indigenous phenomenon, the true-blue offspring of the Western Hemisphere. . . .
He is a self-made writer in the same way that Henry Ford was
a self-made millionaire. On the one hand he is a crass materi-
alist, a greedy consumer of experience, and on the other a
sentimentalist, a half-baked mystic, listening to inward voices
and watching for signs and portents.

A year later – this time in the pages of *Partisan Review* – Rahv
waxed more explicit about American literature's missing ingredient:

The intellectual is the only character missing in the American
novel. He may appear in it in his professional capacity – as
artist, teacher, or scientist – but very rarely as a person who
thinks with his entire being, that is to say, as a person who
transforms ideas into actual dramatic motives instead of merely
using them as ideological conventions or as theories so exter-
nally applied that they can be dispensed with at will. Everything is contained in the American novel except ideas.

What Rahv points toward would become, in the decades that followed, the most significant contribution of immigrant Jewish writers to American literature – namely, a European texture of ideas, of
history, of experience itself. As Irving Howe put it in a 1975 un-
published lecture entitled "The East European Jews and American
Culture": "What then, we may now ask, did the Jews contribute to
American culture? The simplest but fundamental answer is: *they
contributed Europe, they brought the old world back to a country
which had fled from it.*" To be sure, Howe has in mind a rich tapes-
try of names and cultural phenomena: Abraham Cahan, Abraham
Reisen, Henry Roth, the *Di Junge* poets, Jewish Socialists, the
Yiddish theater – indeed, the whole teeming *World of Our Fathers*
(1976) his encyclopedic study so meticulously explores. But at the
time Rahv was arguing for a novel energized by ideas rather than
by the "cult of experience," the landscape of American literature
was dominated by Theodore Dreiser, Thomas Wolfe, Erskine Cald-
well, Sinclair Lewis, John Steinbeck, John Dos Passos, F. Scott

Fitzgerald, William Faulkner, and (perhaps most of all) Ernest Hemingway.

When Saul Bellow's first short story, "Two Morning Monologues," appeared in *Partisan Review* (1941), it had little if any impact on those writers fully credentialed as members of the "cult of experience." But by the time Bellow published his first novel – *Dangling Man* (1944) – there was little doubt about who had thrown a gauntlet to whom:

> There was a time [the novel begins] when people were in the habit of addressing themselves frequently and felt no shame at making a record of their inward transactions. But to keep a journal nowadays is considered a kind of self-indulgence, a weakness, and in poor taste. For this is an era of hardboiled-dom. . . . Do you have feelings? There are correct and incorrect ways of indicating them. Do you have an inner life? It is nobody's business but your own. Do you have emotions? Strangle them. To a degree, everyone obeys this code. . . . [As a result] most serious matters are closed to the hardboiled. They are unpracticed in introspection, and therefore badly equipped to deal with opponents whom they cannot shoot like big game or outdo in daring.

Joseph, the brooding protagonist of *Dangling Man*, has more in common with, say, Dostoyevsky's Underground Man than he does with those in the Hemingway school, whether their name be Natty Bumppo or Nick Adams. In short, Bellow has never been especially shy about demonstrating his kinship either to the Russian novel or to the place of "ideas" in fiction. The trouble with most American writers, he once said in an interview, was that they "imagined they were populists – that is, writing about the people":

> Now most American populist writers of the James T. Farrell or John Steinbeck sort don't bother with ideas very much. Their characters don't have them. If there are ideas, they belong to the whole class of people they are writing about. The individuals themselves can be rather unremarkable, if not down-

right dumb. Now it seemed to me that we had gone as far in America as stupidity would get us. We are living in a very sophisticated society – on the technological side, extremely sophisticated – surrounded by all sorts of curious inventions, and writers still insisted on sitting on the curb playing poker and talking about whores. It seemed to me to be a little artificial. You know, out of loyalty to the people, to cling to your original dumbness. Since it *was* extremely artificial, it was time, I thought, to give it up. I'm not trying to develop a literature for intellectuals. It's just that I'm not afraid of ideas, and when I have to deal with them, I do.

As Bellow's career developed, his brainy protagonists became commonplace, as did the stump speeches they delivered on everything from the decline of the West to long-winded recitations on what women want. One thinks, for example, of Moses Herzog, of Artur Sammler, of Charlie Citrine, of Dean Albert Corde, of Kenneth Trachtenberg – explainers all. Here was the answer to Rahv's plea for the intellectual-as-character with a vengeance, the dream of "Paleface and Redskin" turned into a public success story.

To be sure, Bellow keeps his eggheads on a short comic leash. As Kenneth Trachtenberg, the chief explainer of *More Die of Heartbreak* (1987), puts it:

> If you venture to think in America, you also feel an obligation to provide a historical sketch to go with it, to authenticate or legitimize your thoughts. So it's one moment of flashing insight and then a quarter of an hour of pedantry and tiresome elaboration – academic gabble. Locke to Freud with stops at local stations like Bentham and Kierkegaard. One has to feel sorry for people in such an explanatory bind. Or else (a better alternative) one can develop an eye for the comical side of this.

Indeed, Bellow's richest fictions make it their business to explore "the comical side" of dreamy intellectuals with lives in great disorder. Thus, urban comedians like Moses Herzog or Charlie Citrine are better architects of moral vision than they are accountants of hard fact. Bellow leaves it to others, drawn from a mélange of wacky characters with lowlife expertise, to set his academicians straight. What results are those zigzagging alterations of diction and detail, of the high-flown and the lowlife – all forced to share space in the same thickly textured paragraph – that have become the identifying marks of Bellow's style.

Bookish types have been especially attracted to these sagas of what they take to be fellow sufferers, but Bellow is hardly the paleface Rahv had in mind when he talked about the "thin, solemn, semiclerical culture of Boston and Concord." In fact, Bellow makes a point of flexing his Chicago muscles (and his affection for that city's gritty sense of reality) whenever he gets the chance. One such opportunity was the foreword he wrote for Allan Bloom's *The Closing of the American Mind* (1987). Here, Bellow owns up to the fact that he came to higher learning, as do most modern writers, as an autodidact, and that a novel like *Herzog* (1964) – packed as it was with intellectual history and metaphysical rumination – was designed to make fun of pedantry:

> *Herzog* . . . was meant to be a comic novel: a Ph.D. from a good American university falls apart when his wife leaves him for another man. He is taken by an epistolary fit and writes grieving, biting, ironic, and rambunctious letters not only to his friends and acquaintances, but also to the great men, the giants of thought, who formed his mind. What is he to do in this moment of crisis, pull Aristotle or Spinoza from the shelf and storm through the pages looking for consolation and advice? . . . I meant the novel to show how little strength "higher education" had to offer a troubled man.

Interestingly enough, if Saul Bellow is dogged by charges that he is an elitist, an intellectual, a paleface to the library stacks born, Philip Roth has acquired a considerable reputation as Jewish-American literature's version of the redskin. Granted, forbidden sexual acts and gross offenses against both family order and ordinary decency were hardly new phenomena when Roth burst upon the scene with *Goodbye, Columbus* (1959) or when he brought down the roof ten years later with *Portnoy's Complaint*. What made Roth's situation unique was that his protagonists were Jews and, as Roth put it in *Reading Myself and Others* (1975), "going wild in public was the last thing in the world that a Jew is expected to do – by himself, by his family, by his fellow Jews, and by the larger community of Christians whose tolerance for him is often tenuous to begin with, and whose code of respectability he flaunts or violates at the risk of his fellow Jews' physical and social well-being." But if protagonists like Alexander Portnoy or David Kepesh or Nathan Zuckerman are *vilde chaiyes* (the Yiddish phrase denoting "wild animals"), they are also people who take considerable pains to establish their paleface credentials, their modernist affinities to Henry James, to Franz Kafka, to James Joyce. Pound-for-pound it is not clear that Bellow checks in with more weight of allusion than does Roth, but it is clear that Roth has had a thinner skin where critical opinion is concerned. Bellow has always operated on the general belief that intellectual fashion is precisely that – so much "fashion," so much trendiness; thus, if the New York intellectuals share a common view about thus-and-so, there is probably something wrong with it. Roth, on the other hand, is genuinely divided between wanting to have his satiric egg cookies and hoping that those who have been lambasted will bless his food.

Where, then, does all this get us in terms of our age's palefaces and redskins? Have Rahv's categories – once such vivid emblems of fundamental opposition – become so merged, so homogeneous, that only those who prefer their literature "neat" would continue to use them? After all, what is the point of making an elaborate case that John Updike, a WASP troubled by sexuality and puritanical guilt, represents *the* paleface, and that Norman Mailer, a professional rebel who sounds his barbaric yawp over the assembled throng at meetings of PEN, represents *the* redskin? The bald fact is that most American novelists would squirm if they saw themselves numbered among the palefaces, and this is true whether one has in mind a chest-thumping redskin like Jack Kerouac or a mild-mannered but mischievous academic like John Barth. American novelists may not be as hard-drinking or as hard-travelin' as they once were, but the majority of them still hanker for redder meat and rawer experience – and this includes those more gentrified souls (e.g., Jay McInerney, Brett Easton Ellis) who sidle up to the salad bar in Italian sweaters, pleated pants, and Reeboks, while they fill their plates with tofu and alfalfa sprouts.

The notable exceptions to this generalization, of course, have been the women writers. Rahv was hardly alone in his assumptions that American art should embody the values of masculine culture. The truism might not have seemed worth repeating – as the novelist Joseph Hergesheimer did in a 1921 article entitled "The Feminine Nuisance in American Literature" – but Rahv clearly saw no need to explore the assumptions that lay behind worries about the "feminization" of American literature. Like the poor, the "damned mob of scribbling women" who so infuriated Hawthorne seemed always to be with white, middle-class American authors, and their mere presence always threatened to lower standards and spoil stag parties.

Granted, women novelists could pen powerful bestsellers such as *Uncle Tom's Cabin* or *Gone with the Wind*, but they were seen as belonging to the same paleface camp as the innumerable "poetesses" that Elaine Showalter describes as sporting three names and singing songs "as spontaneous, untaught, and artless as the lark's." Even serious female writers – one thinks of Edith Wharton and Willa Cather, of Sara Teasdale, Edna St. Vincent Millay, and H. D. – found that their considerable reputations could not easily weather modernist storms. Indeed, three years before Rahv published his remarks about palefaces and redskins in the *Kenyon Review*, its editor, John Crowe Ransom, claimed – in an article entitled "The Poet as Woman" – that "A woman lives for love . . . and is indifferent to intellectuality." Male fictionists (including modernist heavy-hitters such as Hemingway and Fitzgerald) dismissed Edith Wharton and even Gertrude Stein as either too decorous or too competitive. "Real" American literature was seen then as clearly a man's game.

In this saga of abuse and neglect, ironies pile atop ironies. For example, Zora Neale Hurston's *Their Eyes Were Watching God* (1937) is now regarded as a canonical text, but its author suffered all the slings and arrows of a "lost" generation of female writers: her books slipped out of print, and one could scour literary histories without so much as encountering her name. When Hurston died in 1960, she was virtually penniless, working as a maid in a welfare home.

But the versions of sisterhood she explored exploded in the decades following her death, beginning with Betty Friedan's *The Feminine Mystique* (1963) and continuing through a wide variety of female writers – Alix Kates Shulman's *Memoirs of an Ex–Prom Queen* (1972), Erica Jong's *Fear of Flying* (1973), Marge Piercy's *Small Changes* (1973), Lisa Alther's *Kinflicks* (1976), Marilyn French's *The Women's Room* (1977), and Toni Morrison's *Song of Solomon* (1977) – suggest something of the range and the power of writing *by* and *for* women.

Moreover, the beat goes on – in the highly politicized poetry and essays of Adrienne Rich, in the historical reevaluations launched by Sandra M. Gilbert and Susan Gubar's *The Madwoman in the Attic* (1979), and in countless number of "gender studies" that currently dominate university-press lists. No doubt Rahv, were he alive, would have to take this energy into account, because it is simply no longer true that our most interesting, most radical "redskins" are always male.

Nonetheless, even if the bulk of our novelists – male and female – are still closer to Barry Hannah than they are to Louis Auchincloss, it is also true that other factors – geographical boosterism, special-interest lobbying – are of greater concern to us now. Whitman made much of his empathetic imagination; he was the poet of men as well as women, of Blacks as well as Whites, of the East as well as the West, of the rich as well as the poor, of the short as well as the tall. Indeed, which American does not fit somewhere under the large, welcoming umbrella of his verse? Today, of course, such chutzpah would surely be met by pinched faces and outrage, especially from those writers who would insist above all else on defining their sexuality, their race, or their ethnic origins by and for themselves. At the same time there are those – I include myself among them – who bristle when the well-meaning turn creative writing into an exercise in affirmative action. Examples of the latter abound, but let me simply cite one – from a questionnaire I received recently from Poets & Writers, an organization that helps struggling artists find outlets for readings and workshops. Before they "book" a writer they need to know if he or she is "(*a*) Black, (*b*) Hispanic/ Latino, (*c*) Puerto Rican, (*d*) Chicano, (*e*) Asian-American, (*f*) Native American, (*g*) Feminist, (*h*) Gay, (*i*) Lesbian, (*j*) Other (Please specify)." For any who might be interested, I was a (*j*). And for my choice of a qualifying adjective to describe the sort of writer I was, I wrote "good." I have, alas, yet to hear from the folks at P&W.

If a case can be made for the continuing good health of terms like paleface and redskin it is likely to be found among those American poets who see themselves as heirs of T. S. Eliot or of William Carlos Williams. For Williams, 1922 – the year Eliot published *The Waste Land* – became the turning point: "Critically Eliot returned us to the classroom just at the moment when I felt that we were on the point of an escape to matters much closer to the essence of a new art form itself – rooted in the locality which should give it fruit." Williams's insistence about "No ideas but in things!" was the battle cry in his long guerrilla warfare against footnotes, against allusion, against myth and symbol, against everything that *The Waste Land* stood for.

Meanwhile, of course, Eliot's magisterial criticism – so rich in the tones of authority, so compelling in its version of canonicity – carried the academic day. "Poetry," Eliot admonished in "Tradition and the Individual Talent," "is not a turning loose of emotion, but an escape from emotion." One suspects that Eliot had in mind Shelley's "I fall upon the thorns of life, I bleed," but that was cold comfort for those who sided with Whitman, with Williams, with other Americans of the chest-thumping sort. Moreover, Eliot commanded larger critical guns. A turn of phrase like "objective correlative" captured academic imaginations in ways that Williams's "variable foot" never quite managed; and when Eliot wrote on behalf of "*Ulysses*, Order and Myth," he was speaking (in barely disguised whispers) about his own method, his own modernist agenda, and his own poem *The Waste Land*. That Eliot's formalism triumphed, and that its very "triumph" – as it moved through stages of incorporation, domestication, and creative exhaustion – was simultaneously the arc of modernism's demise, is by now an overtold tale.

For those poets who encountered Eliot in the classroom – poets of the "middle generation," like Robert Lowell, Delmore Schwartz, and John Berryman – poetry was a sacred calling, one that demanded an unswerving commitment, a scrupulous attention to form, and above all else, intelligence. In other than a modern age, these "poets in their youth" (Eileen Simpson's phrase for the frenetic, bookish life they shared as section men at Harvard) would have been palefaces extraordinaire. But the very pressures that accounted for their brilliance also occasioned patterns of self-destruction and those wildly alternating psychic states we know as manic-depressive. For Lowell, the austere formalism of his early work (e.g., *The Land of Unlikeness*, 1944) contrasts sharply with the confessional openness and radical intimacy of *Life Studies* (1959); for Berryman, there is a world of difference – in texture, in tone, in sheer technique – between his deep identifications with Anne Bradstreet (*Homage to Mistress Bradstreet*, 1956) and his discovery of Henry and the Dream Song. As the myth of democratic mobility would have it, in America one goes from shirt sleeves to shirt sleeves in a mere three generations; in American letters, the progress from paleface to redskin can happen within a lifetime.

In our time, there are those who still tend the paleface flame (e.g., Richard Wilbur, John Hollander, Howard Nemerov), those who continue to have kind words to say about metrics and conventional forms, and who neither apologize nor explain when they are roundly dismissed as "academic poets." But for the most part what we have is a powwow – that is, redskins who run the gamut from those who quietly till Emersonian fields (e.g., A. R. Ammons) to those who have so opened up American poetry that it can, in Louis Simpson's words, "digest / Rubber, coal, uranium, moons, poems."

When Philip Rahv sat down to write about American literature I suspect that he, too, felt it was going through something of a bad patch. The redskin temperament may have carried the day, but Rahv was too cultivated – too European, if you will – to regard the triumph as an unalloyed blessing. Rather than using his culture, the redskin too often allowed it to use him. As Rahv put it: "He is the passive instead of the active agent of the Zeitgeist, he lives off it rather than through it, so that when his particular gifts happen to coincide with the mood of the times he seems modern and contemporary, but once the mood has passed he is in danger of being

quickly discarded." (In our time we know this as the Warhol phenomenon — writers who are famous for fifteen minutes as, say, Tama
Janowitz is currently "famous.") Moreover, Rahv — surrounded
though he was by the evidences of redskin victory — could still
muster up a few kind words on behalf of the past, and about the
contributions that palefaces had made to its richness:

> . . . the paleface, being above all a conscious individual, was
> frequently able to transcend or to deviate sharply from the
> norms of his group, and he is to be credited with most of the
> rigors and charms of the classic American books. While it is
> true, as John Jay Chapman put it, that his culture is "second-
> ary and tertiary" and that between him and the sky "float the
> Constitution of the United States and the traditions and forms
> of English literature" — nevertheless, there exists the poetry of
> Emily Dickinson, there is *The Scarlet Letter*, there is *Moby-
> Dick*, and there are not a few incomparable narratives by
> Henry James.

In this important sense, we have few social critics of Rahv's stature. I say this because there is a mighty difference between Rahv's
considered argument for a novel of ideas, for the intellectual-as-
character and, say, the carping we hear from Kenneth Lynn and
Joseph Epstein on behalf of more representative, altogether nicer
businessmen in literature. As nearly any book reviewer in *Commentary* will tell you, contemporary American literature gives capitalism the bum's rush. That a writer like E. L. Doctorow seems not
to get the message is hardly surprising, especially since the best of
what our neoconservative critics think and say is directed toward
the White House rather than the membership of PEN.

Does this then mean that contemporary palefaces line up on the
Right and contemporary redskins on the Left? I think not, if only
because the equation misses what is essential in Rahv's essay.
Rahv was not pointing to the tensions Leslie Fiedler would later
explore, pitting East against West, North against South. Encrusted
in Fiedler's directional arrows and regional identifications were a
welter of attitudes and postures, histories and antihistories. And
while Rahv might have been sympathetic to arguments that saw the

paleface as the Eastern dandy, the Boston Brahmin, the sophisticated urban-dweller, while viewing the redskin as the Western tough guy, the ring-tailed roarer, the man with mud on his moccasins, I suspect he meant to see these tendencies as psychic divisions within individual writers. By contrast, the polemics that now crackle along the political spectrum from the *Nation* to *New Criterion* divide the world into those mush-headed liberals who talk about government programs and sport "Save the Whales" stickers on their bumpers, and those who take a special delight in playing hardball and knowing how to order expensive wines. None of this, however, tells us much that is important about literature.

By contrast, those who write inside the academy's walls might well argue that the missing character in the American novel is not, as Rahv thought, the intellectual (nor, as Lynn and Epstein hope, the contented capitalist) but, rather, the literary theorist. I should hasten, of course, to add that no literary theorist worth her or his salt would deign to use such old-fashioned words as "novel" or "character." Theory, as critics like Geoffrey Hartman often argue, is where the creative action now resides. Indeed, according to one such prominent "voice" – Marjorie Perloff's – theory is poetry, poetry theory. She says this, by the way, without the slightest hint of irony (yet another outmoded, thoroughly deconstructed term) in illuminating Jacques Derrida's effort in tying language into knots:

> . . . a text like *Glas* is best understood in the context of poetry rather than in the context in which it presently finds itself: the theory course. If this is indeed the case, the next stop – and I have made this experiment with some of my own Contemporary Poetry students, many of whom are poets – is to read *Glas* against, say, John Ashbery's two-column *Litany* or John Cage's "writing through" *Finnegans Wake*, called *Roaratorio*, which uses a kind of odd citational graft and decomposition of word units very much as does Derrida.

At this point we are very far indeed from where we began – far from palefaces and redskins, and more important, far from literature itself.

Fifty years ago, Philip Rahv had fears that American literature might cease to be, that the antipodal forces represented by James and Whitman would never reconcile themselves, much less "finally discover and act upon each other." Indeed, he imagined the richest possibilities for American literature as manifesting themselves in the interplay, and eventual fusion, of paleface and redskin. However delimiting, clumsy, or inappropriate Rahv's central terms may have been, his cultural vision – both in its analysis and its prognosis – merits our continuing attention. For if he could not see far enough into the future to worry about theorists replacing *both* the paleface and the redskin, both James *and* Whitman, he has provided us with a powerful argument for an American literature of mutual enrichment and eventual reconciliation.

The Catcher in the Rye and All: Is the Age of Formative Books Over?

![decorative divider]

> *The best thing, though, in that*
> *museum was that everything always*
> *stayed right where it was. Nobody'd*
> *move. . . . Nobody'd be different. The*
> *only thing that would be different*
> *would be* you.
> Holden Caulfield

I first read these lines about Holden's recollections in anxiety long before I could have identified the allusion to Wordsworth, long before I fell half in love with easeful death and Keats's "Ode on a Grecian Urn," long before I would scrawl "stasis" on the blackboard when lecturing about *The Catcher in the Rye*. And even though I hadn't the foggiest idea about which subway line takes one to the Museum of Natural History, I understood, at sixteen, what Holden was talking about.

In short, there was a time when books – or at least some books – used to matter. One wonders if the same excitements, the same confusions, the same affections persist. Or have formative books gone the way of penny candy and *un*organized baseball games? Perhaps our age is too restless, too sophisticated to suspend its disbelief, much less to sit still long enough to read a book. What follows, then, is an attempt, admittedly autobiographical, to talk about certain connections between reading and culture – not as a "reader-response" theorist, not as a statistics-and-graph sociologist, but rather as one who fell in love with *The Catcher in the Rye* early, and who has been trying to figure out what that has meant ever since.

About some underlying things I am fairly certain: the public indicators that presumably separate one generation in its youth from another (e.g., hairstyles, popular music) are finally less important than the conditions they share. "So much of adolescence," Theodore Roethke once wrote, "is an ill-defined dying, . . . A longing for another time and place,/ another condition." Roethke may have been wrong about the death wish that I, for one, didn't have, but he was dead right about my ill-defined longings. Like Holden, I yearned for a world more attractive, and less mutable, than the one in which we live and are forced to compete. As Holden puts it, with a sadness he does not fully comprehend:

> That's the whole trouble. You can't ever find a place that's nice and peaceful, because there isn't any. You may think there is, but once you get there, when you're not looking, somebody'll sneak up and write "Fuck you" right under your nose. Try it sometime. I think, even, if I ever die, and they stick me in a cemetery, and I have a tombstone and all, it'll say "Holden Caulfield" on it, and then what year I was born and what year I died, and then right under that it'll say "Fuck you." I'm positive, in fact.

That Holden renders a diffuse, universal condition in vivid particulars and that he gives eloquent expression to what I could not have articulated myself are both ways of saying that *The Catcher in the Rye* was, for me, a formative book. Others, no doubt, have candidates of their own: Mother Goose, *Treasure Island*, *The Adventures of Sherlock Holmes* — whatever books they remember as making the imagination's power immanent. But I would argue that our most important formative books are those which lead double lives as cultural statements, fastened as firmly to the here and now as they are to fiction's universals. One wrestles with genuinely formative books, often in ways that are as divided as they are paradoxical. Recalling his own experiences with such books, Lionel Trilling put the matter this way: "The great books taught me, they never made me dream. The bad books made me dream and hurt me; I was right when 4 years ago I said that the best rule-of-thumb for judgment of a good novel or play was – Do you want to be the hero? If you do, the work is bad."

One could claim, and with some justification, that *The Catcher in the Rye* encourages precisely the sort of dreaming and heroic identification that Trilling stands four-square against. Indeed, if moral complexity were the sole issue, one would need look no further than Trilling's *The Middle of the Journey* (1949), an extraordinary novel published a scant two years before *The Catcher in the Rye*. But that said, who would be comfortable in claiming *The Middle of the Journey* as a formative book? To be sure, accessibility is part of the formula, but timing is equally important. A formative book catches its reader at a point when options loom larger than certainties, when an admonition to "change your life" can still have teeth.

For those who grew up in the 1950s, *The Catcher in the Rye* was *the* formative book. My own case, as I struggle to reconstruct it, was one of sharply divided loyalties, of as many repulsions as attractions. A part of me – the part that was reading a book called *On the Road* by an author whose name no one in my literary crowd could even pronounce – wanted, more than anything in the world, to be a beatnik. There were, clearly, no beatniks – at least none in the Kerouac mold – at a cushy joint like Holden's Pencey Prep. My dilemma, I hasten to add, was hardly unusual: formative books come in bunches and, more often than not, send contradictory messages about exactly how one goes about changing one's life. To make matters even more confusing, I kept testing what I read against the life I was actually living. When, for example, ol' Phoebe keeps repeating "Daddy'll *kill* you," I knew, even at sixteen, that this was so much Oedipal bluster. On the other hand, my father really would have leveled me – that is, if I had pissed away even half the money Holden did, or lugged home a single *C*, much less a fistful of *F*'s.

It was Holden's *voice*, rather than his circumstances, that hooked me. Long before the book appeared in its now-familiar bright red, plainly lettered, paperback cover – a dead giveaway that the novel

has become a "classic" and can move off the shelf on its own power –
I kept faith with a well-thumbed copy sporting a picture of an
apple-cheeked, perplexed Holden (wearing his reversed hunting
cap) gazing on the debauchery that was, presumably, New York
City. Apparently, the cover designer sought to blend brows high
and low, the lurid (soft porn à la 1955) with the literary (Daisy
Buchanan eyeballing Manhattan on the dust jacket of *The Great
Gatsby*). Anyway – as Holden might put it – it was the voice that got
me each time I turned to the first page; to get the voice going – or, if
you will, talking – all you had to do was sit back and read:

> If you really want to hear about it, the first thing you'll prob-
> ably want to know is where I was born, and what my lousy
> childhood was like, and how my parents were occupied and
> all before they had me, and all that David Copperfield kind of
> crap, but I don't feel like going into it, if you want to know the
> truth.

To call a Dickens novel crap – and in the same sentence that
heaves in a "lousy" no less! – was to yank literature away from
those who pronounced it "lit-er-ah-tour." Huckleberry Finn warms
up to his task by telling us that Mark Twain "told the truth, mainly,"
but Holden really *does* it, without an apology or so much as a "by
your leave."

At least that was the way I read the book when I was sixteen and
itching to pull down a few vanities myself. In those days Holden
was my "secret sharer," the part of me that knew, down deep, that
whatever Life was, it was decidedly *not* a game: "Game, my ass
[Holden thinks as Spencer hectors him about yet another poor academic performance]. Some game. If you get on the side where all
the hot-shots are, then it's a game all right – I'll admit that. But if
you get on the *other* side, where there aren't any hot-shots, then
what's a game about it? Nothing. No game." To be sure, what
Holden said in bald print I dared only whisper sotto voce. That I
could live with. It was having to share my secret sharer with others
that gave me the gripes. Holden was fast becoming a doppelgänger-
in-residence for an entire generation, including those who pointed
to the obligatory fart-in-the-chapel scene and guffawed. *What right*

have any of you, I wanted to shout, *to think of Holden as a fellow traveler?* Holden would expose *you* as a "secret slob," as a Joe Flit, as a phony.

It took some years before I realized the painful truth – namely, that Holden would probably say the same or worse about me. As Holden would have it, you can count the nonphonies on the fingers of one hand: Allie, his dead brother; Phoebe, his little sister; and of course Holden himself. Everybody else stands either suspect or convicted.

I took a measure of comfort from those passages in which even Holden wonders if he hasn't pulled the self-righteous trigger too quickly. Mr. Antolini, for example, might – or might not – have been a "pervert." What seemed clear enough when Holden was sleeping on Antolini's couch turns complicated when he hits the Manhattan street: ". . . What *did* worry me was the part about how I'd woke up and found him patting me on the head and all. I mean I wondered if just maybe I was wrong about thinking he was making a flitty pass at me. I wondered if maybe he just liked to pat guys on the head when they're asleep. I mean how can you tell about that stuff for sure?"

By this time I was in college: a place where I acquired for the first time that phenomenon known as a roommate, a place where novels like *The Catcher in the Rye* were dissected and placed under critical microscopes. It had taken the New Criticism two decades to trickle down to the small liberal-arts college I attended, but we soon learned to sniff out a paradox or an ambiguity with the best of them. If Salinger hadn't written *The Catcher in the Rye*, one of my professors certainly would have. At least that was the way it seemed, so unerring were they on those quirky Salinger touches we enjoyed without quite knowing how to talk, or write, about them: the kings Jane Gallagher kept in the back row; the question Holden keeps asking about the ducks of Central Park; the whole business of being a "catcher in the rye."

A few years later, while browsing through back issues of *Modern Fiction Studies*, I heard snippets of their dazzling lectures once again, but this time the insights were attached to names I kept bumping into in graduate school: Arthur Mizener, Leslie Fiedler,

Alfred Kazin, James E. Miller, Jr., Frederick L. Gwynn, Joseph L. Blotner – none of whom, I hardly need add, taught at my college. No wonder my professors had wowed the pants off the undergraduates in the third row! Everything they said was safely tucked away in the MLA Bibliography – more critical articles on Salinger than on Hemingway or Fitzgerald or Faulkner. What had started out as an effort to give critical respectability (the Academy's Seal of Approval) to a wildly popular book had turned into a gusher of ink.

In short, the burgeoning Salinger industry did its best, but *The Catcher in the Rye* held up, and together, better than most similarly "saturated" books. After such knowledge, there was – in my case at least – forgiveness. So what if the intimations that would become Holden Caulfield could be unearthed in the wanderings of Odysseus, in the legends surrounding the Grail knights, in Huck Finn's adventures among con-artists and scalawags, in Quentin Compson's obsession with *his* sister? So what if my undergraduate professors took in the best that had been thought and printed about Holden's world and then modified it into their own lectures? Salinger's book was more or less the same book it had always been, and Salinger was, of course, still Salinger.

The truth is, however, that our formative books survive not only subsequent readings but also *ourselves*. In the case of *The Catcher in the Rye*, it even managed to survive what I would not then have believed possible – a time when I no longer counted myself among the Holden-lovers. The well-meaning but ineffectual Mr. Antolini came to strike me as a better model – despite his bows to Wilhelm Steckel and his penchant for stump speeches about the Great Tradition:

. . . you'll find [he tells a shaken Holden] that you're not the first person who was ever confused and frightened and even sickened by human behavior. You're by no means alone on that score, you'll be excited and *stimulated* to know. Many, many men have been just as troubled morally and spiritually as you are right now. Happily, some of them kept records of their troubles. You'll learn from them – if you want to. Just as someday, if you have something to offer, someone will 'earn something from you. It's a beautiful, reciprocal arrangement. And it isn't education. It's history. It's poetry.

Indeed, there will probably come that dreaded day when a bathrobed, bumpy-chested avatar of Mr. Spencer will stare back at me from the mirror. And no doubt I will find him a good deal more sympathetically drawn than I did when I first encountered him reeking of Vicks Nose Drops and made to carry the symbolic role of Sickness Personified.

Teaching Holden's saga in Belgium (under the auspices of a Fulbright grant), I was struck by ironies better than I could have concocted myself, ironies that surely would have made even a Salinger smile. For example, in a university where "Fuck You's" are scrawled on nearly every bathroom wall (graffiti, apparently, requires plaintalking, Anglo-Saxon words; in Belgium, neither French nor Flemish would suffice), my students – reading *The Catcher in the Rye* in the expurgated Penguin edition – had trouble figuring out what the dash in "—— You" stood for. Nonetheless, they fell in love with Holden at first sight. Our most *American* books – everything from *Adventures of Huckleberry Finn* to *Invisible Man* – are as portable as they are powerful. To be sure, my Belgian students had some difficulty understanding the easy arithmetic we make between the American West and the American Dream. When, for example, Holden imagines lighting out for the West, we read the passage with Huck Finn and Frederick Turner firmly in mind:

> Finally, what I decided I'd do, I decided I'd go away. I decided I'd never go home again and I'd never go away to another school again. . . . What I'd do, I figured, I'd go down to the Holland Tunnel and bum a ride, and then I'd bum another one, and another one, and another one, and in a few days I'd be somewhere out West where it was very pretty and sunny and where nobody'd know me and I'd get a job.

My Belgian students knew about the American West by watching "Dallas" and "Dynasty," but they also knew that riding westward – to, say, Ghent – is at best only a two-hour drive from the German

border. In short, they found it hard to make the translation, to feel –
as well as to "know" – just how big, how sprawling, America is.

On the other hand, the things that made Holden "fed up" – the
competitive and the materialistic, as well as, of course, the phony –
struck an easy, sympathetic chord, even in those who found themselves attracted by his description of life among the corporate lawyers: "All you do is make a lot of dough and play golf and play
bridge and buy cars and drink Martinis and look like a hot-shot."
At this point the line between my Belgian students and the American students with whom I'm more familiar began to blur. In roughly
the same way that the well-heeled students at my college in Pennsylvania cheer when the film series shows *Breaking Away*, Belgian
students have no trouble empathizing with Holden while simultaneously keeping their eyes on the main chance. Which is simply to
say that *The Catcher in the Rye* has always had more appeal to
rebels under the skin than to those who actually lugged their failing
transcripts from one prep school to another.

What did not change in my development, however, was my abiding sense of a formative book's continuing power. Granted, I may
have accounted for the power in language that changed with the
decades, I may have shifted this allegiance, altered that loyalty, to
its characters, but the plain truth is Salinger's death-haunted tale
of spiritual yearning, of youthful angst, of dream and nightmare,
has much to do with the how-and-why I plug away at teaching literature to a generation willing to settle for a safe job and a three-piece
suit. I say this not as Mr. Antolini, much less as Holden; not as
Spencer, much less as Salinger. Each of them has become a part of
me in the way that Hester and Huckleberry, together with Madame
Bovary and Leopold Bloom – from other formative books – also
share in the making of my sensibility.

Indeed, the very plurality of formative books is worth speculat-
ing about. There was a time, of course, when the Zeitgeist defined
itself by a single book: the Bible. In our age, however, one might
argue that the itch for *the* formative book has been replaced by a
series of one-night stands: the *I Ching*, the *est Reader*, the *Beverly
Hills Diet Book*. To update Thoreau, the mass of men, and women,

now lead lives of noisy desperation – either screaming "I'm *ter-rrr-if-ic*" at an Amway sales rally or shelling out two-hundred bucks to learn the secrets of Greenspring. In this sense, formative books still abound. People stick them in your face with a missionary zeal not unlike those who waved copies of *The Sayings of Chairman Mao* during the Cultural Revolution. To be sure, the American equivalents are more diversified, more concerned with the pursuit of happiness (defined as everything from inner harmony to outer appearance) than with ideological purity, but they share the general belief that a single book can change things utterly.

Intellectuals, presumably, know better. In the late 1930s Bernard Smith proposed a series of essays in which specialists would choose a work of nonfiction and then show how it had helped to shape the contemporary American mind. After all, as far back as Franklin, we have been makers of lists and lovers of the opinion poll. The *New Republic* warmed to the idea instantly and conducted a lively symposium in its pages. The result is a curious volume entitled *Books That Changed Our Minds*, edited by Malcolm Cowley and Bernard Smith. I say "curious" not because the choices or the discussion about them is odd (e.g., Charles A. Beard on Turner's *The Frontier in American History* or David Daiches on I. A. Richards's *The Principles of Literary Criticism*), but, rather, because the book was published in 1939, even as the world tottered on the brink of a war that would call these academic assessments of culture into deep question. (E. L. Doctorow's 1985 novel *World's Fair* makes a similar point about the celebrated exposition held in New York during the same ominously foreshadowing and pivotal year.)

That the disillusionments of World War I gave birth to the roaring jazz-age 1920s, that the stock market's crash ushered us into the Great Depression, that Hitler's invasion of Poland plunged us into the nightmare of World War II, that Eisenhower's benign, smiling face represented the 1950s in bold relief – these become the convenient shorthand we use to mark the passing of one decade to another. And in large measure, literature seemed to cooperate – the jazz-age flappers of Fitzgerald giving way to the tight-lipped Hemingway heroes of the 1930s, the anxious, world-weary pro-

tagonists of World War II fiction giving way to the spiritually quest-
ing beatniks of the 1950s.

History, of course, does not always cooperate – as we discovered
when, for example, President Kennedy had the doubly bad fortune
to be assassinated in 1963, a year that teetered uneasily between
whatever was left of the somnambulant 1950s and what was yet to
be born as the militant 1960s. Shaped by the art and lives that mattered – in the 1920s by *The Waste Land*, *Ulysses*, *In Our Time*, *The
Great Gatsby*; in the 1930s by Faulkner, Steinbeck, Dos Passos; in
the 1940s by a series of brilliant debuts (Bellow, Mailer, Ellison) –
successive generations of critics held faith with the belief that *their*
decade would also revolve around a handful of Great Books. That it
has, alas, not been so – not in the counterculture's grip on the late
1960s, not during the nondescript 1970s, not as we begin the 1990s –
has come as something of a rude, perplexing shock. Indeed, some
literary critics began to make much ado about the death of fiction:
literature (or, as it came to be fashionably called, "print media in
the linear mode") could no longer compete with film, with television, with the dizzying speed and sheer power of popular culture.
As my students used to put it in the late 1960s: "Literature just
ain't where it's at." Now they tell me it's not "cost effective."

All of which brings me back to *The Catcher in the Rye* and the
Holden Caulfield who roamed Manhattan's unsympathetic streets.
When the novel first appeared in 1951, Holden was seventeen years
old. To imagine him now in *his* early fifties is rather like playing
one of those Victorian parlor games that encouraged speculation
about Ophelia's childhood or about the life Pip and Estella might
lead beyond the final page of *Great Expectations*. The difference, of
course, is that American culture takes its blurrings of Art and Life
quite seriously. Those who find some measure of solace in Jerry
Rubin's turnabout from a Yippie member of the Chicago Seven to a
Yuppie wheeler-dealer on the stock exchange are precisely those
likely to be cheered by the thought of Holden getting his comeup-
pance in a *New Yorker* cartoon.

Mr. Antolini, we remember, had some thoughts about how a
moral uncompromiser like Holden might end up:

"I have a feeling that you're riding for some kind of a terrible, terrible fall. . . . It may be the kind where, at the age of thirty, you sit in some bar hating everybody who comes in looking as if he might have played football in college. Then again, you may pick up just enough education to hate people who say, 'It's a secret between he and I.' Or you may end up in some business office, throwing paper clips at the nearest stenographer. I just don't know. . . ."

To be sure, Mr. Antolini has difficulty imagining Holden *beyond* thirty, but in that regard he is in good American company. Long before the counterculture turned it into the stuff of slogan, Henry David Thoreau made it abundantly clear that he had "lived some thirty years on this planet, and [had] yet to hear the first syllable of valuable or even earnest advice from my seniors." Graybeards – that is, those over thirty – were simply not to be trusted. And in our century, it was F. Scott Fitzgerald, more than any other writer of stature, who equated life in one's thirties with the loss of all that was once held dear: youth, good looks, romance, infinite possibility. As Dexter Green, the protagonist of "Winter Dreams," puts it:

> The dream was gone. Something had been taken from him. . . . He wanted to care, and he could not care. For he had gone away and he could never go back any more. The gates were closed, the sun was gone down, and there was no beauty but the gray beauty of steel that withstands all time. Even the grief he could have borne was left behind in the country of illusion, of youth, of the richness of life, where his winter dreams had flourished.
>
> "Long ago," he said, "long ago there was something in me, but now that thing is gone. Now that thing is gone, that thing is gone. I cannot cry. I cannot care. That thing will come back no more."

No other American writer gave himself so completely to our capacity for Dream, and no writer was better equipped than Fitzgerald to write its Romantic elegy. The wags in Hollywood insisted that he was a "failure at failure," but they were dead wrong. Failure was Fitzgerald's *subject*, just as it is Holden's, just as it is at the center of every sensitive adolescent's complaint. In Theodore Roethke's notebooks – where he did not mince words, where he did not have to curry favor or cover his flanks – he wrote Fitzgerald down in a single, telling sentence: "He was born, and died, a Princeton sophomore."

Holden, of course, remains frozen in his adolescence – in a novel dominated by images of stasis, of freezing (the snowballs he lovingly packs but refuses to throw at cars or fire hydrants because they, too, look "nice and white"; the icy lake of Central Park; the unmoving, Keatsian figures at the museum). And despite our knowing better, we hope against hope that Salinger will also remain the same pipe-smoking, tweed sports-coated, "sensitive" young author who appears on the dust jacket of *The Catcher in the Rye*'s first edition. After all, didn't Salinger himself say, in a contributor's note he wrote for *Harper's* in 1946, "I almost always write about very young people"? And as the Glass family saga unfolded through the 1960s, Salinger kept faith with his manifesto. He wrote *of* the young and *for* the young, so it seemed only fair that the work should continue to be written *by* the young as well. No matter that the mind knows Salinger is now old enough to collect social security; the heart insists that he remain, like his characters, forever fixed, red hunting cap pulled over his ears, the broken pieces of "Little Shirley Beans" in his pockets.

This insistence takes a bizarre, fabulist turn, in W. P. Kinsella's *Shoeless Joe* (1983), a novel in which a cast of improbable characters (e.g., Shoeless Joe Jackson, Moonlight Graham, and J. D. Salinger himself) are assembled at a baseball stadium the protagonist has built on, of all places, an Iowa farm. Baseball is the stuff that American Dreams are made of. When an announcer's "voice" tells Ray Kinsella "If you build it, he will come," Ray turns his bulldozer on the cornfield and – voilà! – Shoeless Joe Jackson appears. And when the voice tells him to "Ease his pain," Kinsella sets off for Salinger's New Hampshire retreat, fully prepared to kidnap him, to drive him across country to Iowa, to "ease his pain."

The rub, of course, is that Salinger's major pain is being pestered by the adoring, the curious, and the downright crazy. As Salinger, the character, puts it:

> Serenity is a very elusive quality. I've been trying all my life to find it. I'm very ordinary. I've never been able to understand why people are so interested in me. Writers are very dull. It's people like you who keep me from achieving what I'm after. You feel that I must be unhappy. A neurotic, guilt-torn artist. I'm *not* unhappy. And I have no wisdom to impart to you. I have no pain for you, unless . . . you and your family were to be plagued with strangers lurking in your bushes, trampling your flower beds, looking in your windows. . . . Once someone stole the valve caps off my jeep. I suppose he sold them or displays them under glass in his library. I don't deserve that!

One could argue that he doesn't deserve a fate as "character" either. After all, a public writer like Norman Mailer leads with a cocked right fist; that he is dragged, kicking and screaming, into Alan Lelchuck's novel, *American Mischief* (1973), has a measure of poetic justice about it. By contrast, Salinger has been eloquent about his "silence." Unfortunately, *any* public figure appears to be fair game in an age that takes a special delight in blurring the distinctions between what we used to know as "fiction" and what we have learned to call "the new journalism."

Part of Salinger's problem, of course, is that he represents a time when *literature* formed literature, when allusions to *Romeo and Juliet* and *Return of the Native*, to *The Great Gatsby* and *A Farewell to Arms*, could be incorporated into the fabric of a novel like *The Catcher in the Rye*. No doubt the deconstructionists would give Holden poor marks, but he is a critic of sorts, nonetheless:

> The book I was reading was this book I took out of the library by mistake. They gave me the wrong book, and I didn't notice it till I got back to my room. They gave me *Out of Africa*, by Isak Dinesen. I thought it was going to stink, but it didn't. It was a very good book. I'm quite illiterate, but I read a lot. . . .

What I like best is a book that's at least funny once in a while. I read a lot of classical books, like *The Return of the Native* and all, and I like them, and I read a lot of war books and mysteries and all, but they don't knock me out too much. What really knocks me out is a book that, when you're all done reading it, you wish the author that wrote it was a terrific friend of yours and you could call him up on the phone whenever you felt like it.

One has the sinking feeling these days that Holden's counterparts at, say, Yale or Johns Hopkins would prefer to shoot the theoretical breeze with imaginative critics rather than with imaginative writers.

Small wonder, then, that most discussions about Salinger's work begin and, all too often, end in nostalgia. As John Romano would have it:

> . . . those who were young and literate in the Eisenhower and Kennedy years can be said to have received such pictures [e.g., Zooey's blue eyes, which were "a day's work to look into"; Franny muttering the Jesus prayer under her breath; Phoebe, in her blue coat, going around and around on the carrousel] with utter credulity and in a state of mind resembling awe. Some of us founded not only our literary taste but also a portion of our identity on Holden Caulfield and Franny Glass: we were smart kids in a dumb world or sensitive kids in a "phony" one, and Salinger was playing our song.

Now it is Ann Beattie who plays somebody else's song in the pages of the *New Yorker*, but the tunes that blare out of her characters' radios sound unfamiliar, and the characters themselves strike us as inarticulate. Allusions shrink to last season's television schedule, a movie, a "hot" rock album. To be sure, people in *New Yorker* stories still suffer angst, but if technique is still style, theirs is a threadbare version.

In this sense, Jay McInerney's *Bright Lights, Big City* (1984) is also a book about the glitz, the fashion, the *tempora et mores* of Manhattan's faster lanes. As Holden's saga is simultaneously a satiric attack and a cautionary tale, so too is McInerney's. Moreover, behind *Bright Lights, Big City*'s smart talk about Bolivian Marching Powder (i.e., cocaine) and its quick studies in SoHo eccentricity lies a long history of American writers who equated the City with infinite possibilities, and who surrendered themselves to its Dream: the Hawthorne of "My Kinsman, Major Molineux," the Whitman of *Leaves of Grass*, the Dos Passos of *Manhattan Transfer*, and of course the Fitzgerald of *The Great Gatsby*.

Bright Lights, Big City has its Salingeresque connections – in the way, for example, that its protagonist describes one woman as having "cheekbones to break your heart" or another as having a voice "like the New Jersey State Anthem played through an electric shaver" – and, more important, in the way it has apparently been adopted by many as an etiquette book for the eighties. But the *real* connections, the shivery ones, are to F. Scott Fitzgerald. Jay McInerney is "news" – whether the news be about the $200,000 he received to turn *Bright Lights, Big City* into a Hollywood screenplay or accounts of his partying with Mick Jagger. He is sleek, handsome, barely past thirty, and an "established author" on the strength of one book. In short, McInerney is a secret sharer with the Fitzgerald who rocketed to stardom, literary and otherwise, by way of *This Side of Paradise*.

But this is also a case in which history repeats itself with a difference. If Fitzgerald's account of "parlor snakes" and "petting parties," of Princeton undergrads who got "boiled" at dances and vamps who had been kissed by "dozens of boys," was both a sensation and a Victorian shocker, McInerney's guided tour of Manhattan night life will, no doubt, strike even the most permissive parent as an updated, and upsetting, equivalent:

You are not the kind of guy who would be at a place like this at this time of morning. But here you are, and you cannot say that the terrain is entirely unfamiliar, although the details are fuzzy. You are at a nightclub talking to a girl with a shaved head. The club is either Heartbreak or the Lizard Lounge. . . . Somewhere back there you could have cut your losses, but you rode past that moment on a comet trail of white powder and now you are trying to hang on to the rush.

Shimmering surface details are, of course, only a small part of what make Fitzgerald and McInerney such fascinating doppelgängers. At a deeper, more significant level, what they share is a vision about failure, about breakdown, about crack up. With an *i* dotted here, a *t* crossed there, this passage from *Big Lights, Big City* might have been lifted from the Old Master:

> You started on the Upper East Side with champagne and un-limited prospects, strictly observing the Allagash rule of per-petual motion: one drink per stop. Tad's mission in life is to have more fun than anyone else in New York City, and this involves a lot of moving around, since there is always the like-lihood that where you aren't is more fun than where you are. You are awed by his strict refusal to acknowledge any goal higher than the pursuit of pleasure. You want to be like that. You also think he is spoiled and dangerous. His friends are all rich and spoiled. . . .

This is the sort of world my students can "relate" to, the sort of world they hope to discover themselves after graduation. That most of them are not yet reading the book McInerney has written is a matter we will take up – with mixed results, I suspect – when *Bright Lights, Big City* elbows its way into the syllabus for English 263: Contemporary American Novel. Then I will tell them that, in Holden Caulfield's day, the Joe Flits wore tattersall vests and gray suiting; now they deck themselves out in designer jeans and Ree-boks. What doesn't change, however, is the single word required to write both down: *phony.*

No doubt my students will shake off what I say about *their* cur-rent favorite, and perhaps they should. After all, when those in the know about postmodernist fiction wag their fingers at *The Catcher in the Rye* and call it "counterfeit," I continue to listen to the voices that mattered, and that still matter – namely those in Salinger's novel. Given the choice of being "suckered in" by fiction or by a critic of fiction, I know where to take my stand. And I hope that my students do too.

What worries me, however, is not so much that a hot book like *Bright Lights, Big City* may or may not weather the storms of time (few novels do), but that the notion of formative books per se may be sunk. Our culture moves with a speed as blinding as it is fickle. If we have not quite reached Andy Warhol's dream of everyone in America being famous for fifteen minutes, we are coming dangerously close. Even the most "with-it" of my students would squirm if they had to read yellowing copies of *People* magazine or sit through reruns on MTV. That, they would argue, is so much *history*, which Henry Ford, in another time and place, called so much bunk.

Rather than formative experiences, contemporary culture demands *new* ones – slicker, trendier, and (most important of all) disposable. *Bright Lights, Big City* – sandwiched uneasily between a film like *St. Elmo's Fire* and the current Land's End catalogue – is simply the latest, most interesting example of "This is how the world goes. . . ." I take some consolation in reminding myself that this, too, shall pass – and no doubt with deliberate speed – but I take a larger measure of satisfaction from my certain knowledge that, despite everything, and in his fifties, Holden Caulfield still has an honored place in the minds of what might well be the last generation to have formed its imagination, its sense of who we were, from the pages of a formative book.

Versions of Comic Relief

The first article in this section – "Comedy and Cultural Timing: The Lessons of Robert Benchley and Woody Allen" – argues that our national appetite for earnestness is very strong. Indeed, some readers might even detect a residual Puritanism in the essays that opened this volume, and they would not be entirely wrong. But humor forces all of us to put things into perspective; it helps us "bear the bad news." Humor also suggests – sometimes gently, sometimes via the uncompromising hand of satire – that the "bad news" might not be quite as bad as we had imagined it to be. For if it is true that we are currently going through something of a bad patch where "serious" literature is concerned, one could argue that the traditions of American humor are alive and well.

The respective careers of Robert Benchley and Woody Allen illustrate the last point impressively. Both began as writers for the *New Yorker* magazine (arguably the most important venue for humor, then and now, in American culture), and both pursued careers in Hollywood. That Allen manages to flourish on the silver screen – the very place that Benchley found so lacking in artistic possibilities – is additional testimony to our hipper times and our humorous customs.

Lenny Bruce is another story altogether. If he is not quite the capital-A Artist or martyred giant that his boosters would make of him, he certainly broke new comedic ground and influenced a whole range of comics who now work – relatively uncensored – in comedy clubs such as Catch a Rising Star or The Improv, as well as on television (especially cable) and increasingly in feature-length films.

For cultural critics, then, humor is a necessary dosage of "comic relief," as well as a phenomenon worthy of study in its own right.

As humorists from Benjamin Franklin to Mark Twain have demonstrated, America has always been good for a laugh – and whether one prefers Russell Baker or Garrison Keillor, Mel Brooks or Woody Allen, the essential American situation has not changed.

Comedy and
Cultural Timing:
The Lessons of
Robert Benchley and
Woody Allen

s any stand-up comic will tell you, the secrets of comedy
are timing, timing, and timing. Mark Twain, for example,
knew how to convulse an audience by taking it slow.
Mighty slow. His poker face, his omnipresent cigar, and
his exaggerated Southern drawl were the props that informed
and sustained hilarious bits such as "Jim Baker's Blue-Jay Yarn"
and "Jim Blaine and His Grandfather's Old Ram." Long before
Jack Benny had his radio audience fiddling at the dials as he pon-
dered the question "Your money, or your life," Mark Twain knew
how effective – and how funny – silence could be.

But there is timing of another sort, one that speaks to the Zeitgeist as much as it does to the individual performer. What tickled
an eighteenth-century Colonial funnybone would have seemed very
tame indeed to the audience who howled at the antics of an un-
reconstructed nineteenth-century Southerner like Sut Luvingood –
and for those of us who have learned to live under the shadow of the
Bomb, even Sut is no match for "sick" comics such as Lenny Bruce
or the motley crew of "Saturday Night Live." Granted, our most
enduring humorists have also understood that American culture
wears a Janus face: its official side is earnest, hard-working, serious, and sober; its "flip side" is precisely that – flip, irreverent,
just aching to knock the Protestant ethic into a cocked hat.

Thus has it been – at least since the War of Independence, if not
longer. The Election Day sermon, the Chautauqua lecture, the

after-dinner speech, the "educational toy" – all these bear eloquent witness to a Puritanism that remains as persistent as it is nagging. No matter how desperately we pretend otherwise, our official culture continues to believe that idle hands and upturned grins are the devil's workshop, and that only the microwave oven or the harvest-gold blender behind door number 3 justifies one's dressing up as a radish and squealing uncontrollably on "Let's Make a Deal." Whatever doesn't manifestly teach or manifestly preach falls automatically into the large catchall that includes the frivolous, the escapist, and (not least) the *merely* humorous.

It is hardly surprising, then, that the jeremiad has had such a long, successful run in America, or that an incarnation such as Allan Bloom's *The Closing of the American Mind* (1987) should wind up on the best-seller list. As Bloom would have it, there are dangers to high seriousness everywhere: in our lack of critical standards, in our worship of a mushy-headed relativism, in our vulgarized notions of nihilism. One sees sure signs of decay, he argues, in the sheer number of colleges and universities racing to establish "Women's Studies" programs, in the rock music that teenagers blast through their Walkmen, and in such unlikely places as the films of Woody Allen.

Allan Bloom, of course, means to bash them all, but it is his attack on Woody Allen that speaks most directly to our culture's mixed feelings about comedy. According to Bloom,

> Woody Allen's comedy is nothing but a set of variations on the theme of the man who does not have a real "self" or "identity," and who feels superior to the inauthentically self-satisfied people because he is conscious of his situation and at the same time inferior to them because they are "adjusted."

In short, Allen makes us feel comfortable with our nihilism, and for this sin Bloom can offer book lists but no forgiveness: "Woody Allen really has nothing to tell us about inner-directedness. Nor does David Riesman [in *The Lonely Crowd*] nor, going further back, does Eric Fromm. One has to get to Heidegger to learn something serious about the grim facts of what inner-directedness might really mean." Reading such strident judgments, one begins to suspect that the Allan with the problem is Bloom rather than Woody.

Paradoxically, nothing makes Americans squirm more than the imposition of an official, pinch-faced culture. What Allan Bloom demonstrates when he blathers on about a film like *Zelig* is precisely what H. L. Mencken once defined as the Puritan temper – namely, a deep suspicion that somebody, somewhere, is having a good time. It has been with us, in one form or another, from the days when Thomas Morton established his Maypole at Merry Mount in 1628 (only to have Governor John Endicott transmogrify it, in Hawthorne's version of the tale, into a "whipping-post") to *Animal House* and the latest round of efforts to exile fraternities from college campuses.

Comedy, as the title of Harry Levin's 1987 study points out, is an unending battle between *Playboys and Killjoys*, between dionysian revel and apollonian restraint. Historically, American humorists have been especially attracted to those forms which pit horse sense against book learning, the person of few, ironic words (*eiron*) against the pedantic person of many (*alazon*). Small wonder, then, that the stuffy lecture gone haywire has become such a staple ingredient of American humor. It is not merely that we prefer recess to long division or grammar drills, not merely that democracy and anti-intellectualism are more closely related than we would like to admit; rather, it is that we are deeply divided about the work ethic that is both the cause of America's greatness and the frequent occasion for its psychic woe.

Moreover, American humorists have long played on the ambivalence that causes self-made millionaires to endow colleges and universities at the same time that they are deeply suspicious about the education going on in the buildings they have built. As in the cartoons of mad scientists cackling over their steaming beakers or Viennese psychiatrists who are clearly crazier than their patients, humor has always domesticated what we fear or feel we have an obligation to hold in reverence – and nowhere is this truer than in our culture's protracted, undeclared war against "culture" itself.

Indeed, pulling down privilege and intellectual vanity has a long, distinguished history in American humor. At the tender age of sixteen, Benjamin Franklin (writing under the disguise of Silence Dogood) had this to say about Harvard College:

> . . . I reflected in my Mind on the extream Folly of those Parents, who, blind to their Childrens Dulness, and insensible of the Solidity of their Skulls, because they think their Purses can afford it, will needs send them to the Temple of Learning, where, for want of a suitable Genius, they learn little more than how to carry themselves handsomely, and enter a Room genteely, (which might as well be acquir'd at a Dancing-School,) and from whence they return, after Abundance of Trouble and Charge, as great Blockheads as ever, only more proud and self-conceited.

Franklin speaks to the leather-apron crowd, to those who work with their hands and who have learned to value common sense. By contrast, nineteenth-century American humorists tended to choose up sides: some, like John Kendrick Bangs and Eugene Field, following the lead of Oliver Wendell Holmes and his influential *The Autocrat of the Breakfast-Table* (1858); others, such as Artemus Ward, Petroleum Vesuvius Nasby, Josh Billings, and (most spectacularly) Mark Twain cast their lot with the "lowfalutin." In large measure, those with a taste for learned allusions and sophisticated wordplay (the former) did not keep company with those who thought that fractured misspellings were the stuff of which "phunny phellows" are made.

But as Norris W. Yates points out in *Robert Benchley* (1968), our century was destined to see these divided humorous streams mingle – and then learn to coexist:

> . . . a typical page in *Puck* at the turn of the century includes an attack in dialect on the Democratic Party, and a cartoon featuring the "Gibson girl," one of the favorite archetypes of genteel humor. All three of the leading comic weeklies, *Puck*, *Judge*, and *Life*, as well as the leading comic monthly, *Vanity Fair*, accepted numerous contributions both from the cracker-barrel writers and their more polished brethren.

Regional humorists – whether they hung their bowler hats in Brahmin Boston or lit out for the "unsivilized" territories of the Old Southwest – were no match for the homogenization that would come with the territory of national magazines and big-city newspapers, and later with radio, motion pictures, and television.

By focusing on 1910 – the year that Mark Twain died, the year that T. S. Eliot wrote "The Love Song of J. Alfred Prufrock" and graduated from Harvard College – one can see the shift from the Southwestern Old to the Modernist New. Virginia Woolf claimed that this was the year in which "human nature changed," and given the impact of such cultural explosions as Roger Fry's postimpressionist exhibition or the premiere of Stravinsky's "The Firebird" ballet, who could say that she was wrong? By any measure, 1910 was a watershed year. I would argue, moreover, that the apparently random events that clustered together under the umbrella of that date point toward a general direction in modern life – namely, the need to take confusion, ineptitude, and sheer helplessness into full account. Mark Twain's satiric deflations of the boast-and-brag associated with ring-tailed roarers (see, for example, "The Raftsmen's Passage" in *Adventures of Huckleberry Finn*) would no longer suffice – not only because timid people, rather than colorful characters named Sudden Death and General Desolation, now walked the streets of New York City, but also because the very notion of the "boast" had been brought into serious question. In short, the time was ripe for the humorous protagonist to take on a new, contemporary posture.

| | |

Enter Robert Benchley. In 1910, he was elected to the Harvard *Lampoon*'s board of editors and began cracking up the Harvard houses with comic monologues that were the essence – albeit, in embryonic form – of what would evolve as the "Little Man," our century's most enduring comic persona. By all accounts, Benchley's Harvard antics were the stuff of legend. He traveled "Through the Alimentary Canal with Gun and Camera" on a number of occasions; once he recruited a local Chinese laundryworker to appear at a Harvard football banquet as Professor Soony of the Imperial University of China and to lecture those assembled (via Benchley's "translation") on the bogus history of Chinese football; and his Ivy Oration at the commencement exercises for the Class of 1912 raised the loopy non sequitur to a high art. Perhaps most impressive of all, he was, even then, regarded as such a wit that Harvard's president insisted on not being given the formidable task of following Benchley's after-dinner remarks. Granted, such high jinks did not get Benchley a professorship at Harvard or elsewhere, but they did lead, in something of an extended arc, to a chair at the Algonquin Round Table.

Robert Benchley as our century's first Little Man? Those old enough to know – and indeed, that was part of the joke – know that Benchley was hardly a little man physically. He tended toward the corpulent, a fitter subject for a role as Daddy Warbucks than a shrimp. At the same time, of course, his mustache and oddly undersized head – perched as they were atop a pear-shaped physique – could be played to comic advantage, and that is precisely what Benchley, from the beginning, did. He perfected the role of the man who ought to be in control but obviously isn't, and as the rattle lines grew across his brow, his audiences could feel, simultaneously, the identification and the distance that make for comic art. Benchley's size became a comment on a world where bulk no longer mattered, where taxi cabs regularly sped by as if he were not there, umbrella raised and overcoat bursting at the buttons. He suffered the twentieth century as New Yorkers knew it on a daily basis, even if they made comfortable salaries and tried hard to live orderly lives. The madness welling up from the sidewalks – rather than his shirt size – is what made Benchley's Little Man *little*.

Like most humorists, Benchley began as a counterpuncher, which means that he kept his eyes and, more important, his ears fixed on those elements of the mainstream culture most susceptible to comic exaggeration. For Benchley, the parody lecture was an especially appealing form, not only because it had a long, durable tradition in American humor, but also because he could give it a distinctly modern application. Rather than the droll, poker-faced platform speakers pioneered by Artemus Ward and perfected by

Mark Twain, Benchley's lecturers were usually nervous, bumbling types who got their facts confused and their illustrations out of order. Such "lectures" were comic accidents waiting to happen.

Which brings us to "The Treasurer's Report," a piece of funny business that has an honored place in the Benchley apocrypha. Benchley scholars generally agree that this signature piece marked the culmination of an amateur career and the beginning of what was to be a long professional run (273 performances in the *Music Box Revue* of 1923, followed by a film version five years later). There is less agreement about Benchley's claim that he simply showed up to an audition for the Algonquin group's *No Sirree!* revue of April 22, 1922, without the faintest idea, much less with a script, of what he might do. Twain's platform performances had been the result of painstaking care and multiple drafts; by contrast, Benchley's parodic lectures left wide spaces open for improvisation. Indeed, his persona as the anxious, inept lecturer may well have masked something of the same anxiousness in Benchley himself. The result was a humor of high risk, a version of what those in international diplomacy like to call "brinksmanship."

But it is worth remembering that, by 1922, Benchley had been at it for more than a decade, and that if he did not have the exact wording, he certainly had the essential music. Benchley was, in fact, a funny fellow, without the need for fractured misspellings or a large-budget production. He knew that "sheer madness is, of course, the highest brow in humor," and his dreams were filled with darkly comic, very funny stuff – whether it be a nightmare in which he imagines himself in a boxing ring "facing the better of the two men" or a fantasy in which he is choked to death by his necktie: "After two minutes of this mad wrenching one of three things happens – the tie rips, the collar tears, or I strangle to death in a horrid manner with eyes bulging and temples distended, a ghastly caricature of my real self." All he really needed to make his Little Man come alive was a lectern or a desk, and of course, some occasion for him to clear up those sticky matters that so bedevil us. As one of his representative sketches begins: "It is high time that someone came out with a clear statement of the international financial situation." The premise is as fresh, as fraught with comic potential, as anything Russell Baker might write in next week's *New York Times*. And although I have an enormous admiration for Baker's columns, I also suspect that he would be hard pressed to write a paragraph as lucid, or as funny, as the one Benchley crafted years ago:

> Now there is a certain principle which has to be followed in all financial discussions involving sums over one hundred dollars. There is probably not more than one hundred dollars in actual cash in circulation today. That is, if you were to call in all the bills and silver and gold in the country at noon tomorrow and pile them up on a table, you would find that you had just about one hundred dollars, with perhaps several Canadian pennies and a few peppermint life-savers. All the rest of the money you hear about doesn't exist. It is conversation money. When you hear of a transaction involving $50,000,000 it means that one firm wrote $50,000,000 on a piece of paper and gave it to another firm, and the other firm took it home and said, "Look, Momma, I got $50,000,000!" But when Momma asked for a dollar and a quarter out of it to pay the man who washed the windows, the answer probably was that the firm hadn't got more than seventy cents in cash.

Versions of Benchley's Little Man were destined to become a staple of twentieth-century American humor, popping up as Chaplin's little tramp and as James Thurber's dreamy Walter Mitty, in the delusions of S. J. Perelman's wackier protagonists (especially when they imagine themselves looking like Ronald Coleman and dancing like Fred Astaire – only to discover that they were eons away from either), and most recently, in the benighted gaze and underscale frame of Woody Allen.

Benchley and his cronies (i.e., Dorothy Parker, F. P. Adams, Alexander Woollcott, George S. Kaufman, Ring Lardner) became the American version of, say, the town wits in eighteenth-century London. They were quick and sharp and, perhaps most important of all, eminently quotable in an age when sophistication mattered and when newspaper columns like "The Conning Tower" carried their caustic, urbane humor well beyond the doors of the Algonquin Hotel. The games the Algonquin wags played were hardly the mindless banter of shows like "Hollywood Squares." When, for example, an overbearing young man tried to ingratiate himself with Dorothy Parker by announcing, "I can't bear fools," Parker shot back: "That's queer. Your mother could." Alexander Woollcott was even worse, as a female guest to the Round Table discovered when he glowered at her and announced in richly rounded Woollcottian tones, "You are married to a cuckold."

But two cultural institutions made the Big Difference for Benchley. One was the *New Yorker* magazine (founded in 1925); the other was Hollywood.

In the years before the *New Yorker*, Benchley often dreamed of writing for a *real* humor magazine, one that would be independent of advertisers and that would bring together under one cover the best work being done by the best humorists. To be sure, Benchley had been associated with the other humor magazines of his day: the old *Vanity Fair*, the old *Life*. Indeed, he brought a fully realized Little Man to Harold Ross's the *New Yorker* offices, but the plain fact is that Benchley had at last found his base. Once again, cultural timing proved to be crucial, as the *New Yorker* magazine became increasingly important while the other humor magazines grew dusty and were eventually discontinued.

As James Thurber once pointed out (with nearly equal doses of admiration and exasperation), for the person beating his or her brains out trying to write a 2,000-word comic sketch, there was always "the suspicion that a piece he has been working on for two long days was done much better and probably more quickly by Robert Benchley in 1924." My hunch is that Thurber was right about the former: nobody could beat Benchley when it came either to asking the great nonsense questions of our time ("Do Insects Think?") or to putting his finger on the irritations that come with modern domestic life ("This is written [one piece begins] for those men who have wives who are constantly insisting on their asking questions of officials"). But I also suspect that Thurber was dead wrong when he imagined that such sketches came easily. Benchley worked hard to create the illusion that his humor was turned out casually; indeed, the same thing could be said of S. J. Perelman, of E. B. White, and of Thurber himself.

But the Benchley who, in effect, made the *New Yorker*'s brand of modern humor possible – in roughly the same way that Faulkner made modern writing about the South newly possible or that Bellow showed us how to write about modern Jewish-Americans – was the same Benchley who found himself delimited by the strictures of the 2,000-word sketch and overshadowed by the monuments of literary modernism. After all, we are more likely to associate the year 1925 with the publication of F. Scott Fitzgerald's *The Great Gatsby* or Ernest Hemingway's *In Our Time*, with John Dos Passos's *Manhattan Transfer* or Theodore Dreiser's *An American Tragedy* than with the founding of the *New Yorker*. Scope, ambition, depth – these are the criteria for greatness we have been taught to recognize and to revere; collections of humorous sketches (even when, as in Benchley's case, there are some thirteen of them) do not – indeed, *cannot* – pass muster. We may have been amused, but (to twist Queen Victoria's words) we are not impressed. One looks in vain to find Benchley selections in today's standard anthologies of American literature, or even to see his name on college course syllabi.

Yet, one could argue that some of the best inch-by-inch writing done in our century – writing that has had a permanent effect on the precision, the clarity, and the cadence of American prose – was done by the *New Yorker* humorists who labored on this side of the Atlantic rather than by expatriates who airmailed the latest modernist news from Paris. Unfortunately, Benchley, who wanted nothing more than to be a "real" writer, was convinced that he had missed the boat, that he had squandered his talent. He ended his days feverishly working on a book about British literature's Queen Anne period. Presumably, *that* would be worthy, substantial, serious. It would be, in short, everything that humor wasn't.

Modern humor needs its trouble, not only as a subject matter but also as an interior condition both of the comic persona and of the anxious person scribbling away behind the mask. For the Benchley who set his table and filled his martini shaker by recounting seemingly endless combinations of the Little Man's misadventures, there must have been that awful moment when he wondered if more were not less. Hollywood – where he churned out some forty-eight short subjects (ten- to twenty-minute films designed to pad a "double bill" in the days when people expected their full fifty cents' worth at the Bijou) and appeared in, or collaborated on, nearly as many feature-length films – spared him the need for wonder: he *knew* that any similarity between the Joe Doakes of the Hollywood short subject and the Little Man at his finely honed best was merely coincidental. Unfortunately, Benchley could not imagine a Hollywood with wider, much less deeper, possibilities – and such a Hollywood, at least for humorists, did not then exist.

Benchley's is a case in which ironies pile up until the spirit breaks. He was taller and certainly more portly than most, but he could never quite escape from the constraints of the brief sketch or the short subject. He served long and well (1929–1940) as the *New Yorker*'s drama critic, but the general public thought of him mainly as an actor. Benchley spent a good deal of time spending Hollywood's money and then gumming the hands that had fed him. "I am not an actor," he once wrote Harold Ross, but then he added poignantly, "I don't know what I am."

| | |

The respective careers of Robert Benchley and Woody Allen invite, even beg for, comparison. After all, both humorists are chroniclers of the Little Man's continuing misadventures; both explore the wide gaps between the way life is and the way it ought to be; and most important of all, both are inextricably connected with the *New Yorker* magazine and the silver screen. But if the general outline of Allen's career suggests a case of Benchley's history repeating itself, their essential differences – in ethnicity, in social class, and in cultural timing – are crucial.

Benchley came to humor as a social insider: he was a New England WASP who prepped at Philips Exeter Academy before trying out his humorist's wings at Cambridge. Indeed, only an insider – somebody who knew Old School ties, jackets, and values as intimately as Benchley did – could lay the cornerstone of the dementia praecox school in Harvard Yard. By contrast, Woody Allen springs from the noisy, yoo-hooing world of Brooklyn. His childhood memories are filled with people who shouted rather than talked, who ended their sentences with exclamation points, and who could do neither without waving their hands. Such a world – by degrees combative and warm, ebullient and anxious – tends to divide itself between those who reach over others for a ketchup bottle at the luncheonette counter and those "others" who get knocked off their stools in the process. Woody Allen has emerged as the latter group's patron saint and most articulate voice.

That one could count Woody Allen as yet another modern humorist with trouble hanging from his sleeve is true enough, but he strikes us as adding up to more than that formulation. For one thing, his *tsoris* has a metaphysical dimension we recognize like a thumbprint: "The universe is merely a fleeting idea in God's mind – a pretty uncomfortable thought, particularly if you've just made a down payment on a house." If Benchley has a fondness for following the *non sequitur* until it goes "off the wall," Allen likes to muse in juxtapositions. The result is a prose style in which airy ideas and gritty urban details are forced to share floor space in the same paragraph, and often on opposing sides of a semicolon.

Allen's sketches, like Benchley's, tend to begin in parody, which is to say that Allen is also an effective counterpuncher. But whereas Benchley had no clear predecessors, Allen labors under the long shadows cast by Benchley, Thurber, and Perelman. Consider, for example, this paragraph from Allen's "A Look at Organized Crime" (from *Getting Even*, 1972):

> In 1921, Thomas (The Butcher) Covello and Ciro (The Tailor) Santucci attempted to organize disparate ethnic groups of the underworld and thus take over Chicago. This was foiled when Albert (The Logical Positivist) Corillo assassinated Kid Lipsky by locking him in a closet and sucking all the air out through a straw.

On its most immediate, most recognizable level, Allen is having some fun at the expense of what had been a popular television show – "The Untouchables" – and the spate of books about the Mob it

inspired; on other fronts, he cannot quite resist the impulse to jux-
tapose a nickname we expect with one we don't. But he continues
with a level of allusion many may have missed, especially those
who knew Allen from his days as a Greenwich Village nightclub
comic rather than as a writer firmly grounded in the *New Yorker*
tradition:

> Then there was Aunt Sarah Shoaf, who never went to bed at
> night without the fear that a burglar was going to get in and
> blow chloroform under her door through a tube. To avert this
> calamity — for she was in greater dread of anesthetics than of
> losing her household goods — she always piled her money,
> silverware, and other valuables in a neat stack just outside
> her bedroom, with a note reading: "This is all I have. Please
> take it and do not use your chloroform, as this is all I have."

Aunt Sarah Shoaf is, of course, one of the lovable eccentrics who
made James Thurber's childhood in Columbus, Ohio, so ripe for
the *New Yorker*'s picking.

Like Benchley, like Thurber, like Perelman, Allen cannot re-
count his complicated griefs without making them seem comic. But
Allen has some advantages that his predecessors did not. He plays
to a hipper house, one he describes as "born after Nietzsche's edict
that 'God is dead,' but before the [Beatles'] hit recording 'I Wanna
Hold Your Hand.'" Also, Allen broke in his version of the sad-
sack-as-schlemiel at a cultural moment when ethnicity was becoming a box-office "plus" rather than the marginal minus it had always
been considered. If radio tended to obliterate regional dialects, ho-
mogenizing our speech until the diction of CBS announcers became
the American equivalent of the King's English, then movies (and
later, television) turned a country of small towns into a nation of
urban states.

To be sure, the process I'm describing happened so slowly, so
subtly, that it defies precise dating. Nor is the greater receptiveness,
the more culturally hospitable climate I am trying to describe, lim-
ited to American humorists. For example, what cluster of events accounts for the 1964 revival, and the subsequent popularity, of *Call
It Sleep* (1934), Henry Roth's lyrical novel about growing up amid

the squalor and the terrors of New York's immigrant Lower East Side? One would *like* to give the obvious answer – namely, that it's a first-rate book – but popular taste is more complicated. Without a different literary context that now included the work of Saul Bellow, Bernard Malamud, and another Roth named Philip; without a cultural moment in which one didn't have to be Jewish to enjoy Levy's rye bread or to know a few Yiddish words; without, in short, the 1960s as they were, Henry Roth's novel might have continued its long, uninterrupted sleep. Similarly, even after Benchley and even after Chaplin's comedies, a film as aggressively ethnic as *Annie Hall* (1977) would have been impossible in the 1930s.

Roughly the same cultural changes affected what a stand-up comic could, or could not, do behind a mike. If Woody Allen hadn't bumbled along in the 1960s with his urban (read "Jewish") neurosis and his sad, bespectacled *punim*, somebody would surely have invented him. The era of the Borscht Belt gag ("I spent a thousand dollars to have my nose fixed, and now my brain won't work" – *bup bup bup*) was over. By contrast, Allen's characteristic shrugs and quivers, his obsessive worries and pervasive guilts, his hesitant pauses and equally hesitant voice, were just right for the *Playboy* crowd. Treating his audience as if it were his analyst, Allen would confess, "I don't believe in an afterlife, although I plan to bring a change of underwear." Or he would offer his remembrances of neuroses past: "When we played softball, I'd steal second, then feel guilty and go back." As one critic of the Village scene of late 1960s put it: "The futzing around Allen did onstage was the gestalt of a comedic antihero . . . true neurotica."

To be sure, Allen's onstage "futzing" is now an "on-screen" dimension of the Allen persona, but for those curious about its embryonic form, the essence of his nightclub work (1964–1968) is preserved on five long-playing phonograph records. More important, however, is the very fact that comedy albums now exist, and that they are such hot sellers. By contrast, the Benchley who performed before he could be preserved by modern technology trod his hour upon the revue stage and essentially was then heard no more. He came to radio only at the end of his career and missed out on television altogether.

The *New Yorker* magazine was another matter. In its venerable pages Benchley was the legend, and Allen the upstart. But, once again, Allen could reap certain cultural benefits – in this case, an atmosphere heavy with the results of some twenty years of mass higher education. In short, he could depend on a readership that had gone to college, that had domesticated Freud and had a feel for the Kafkaesque, that had taken courses in the modern novel and seen foreign films with subtitles. In short, he could count on readers ready to laugh at passages like the following:

> Now Cloquet stepped closer to Brisseau's sleeping hulk and again cocked the pistol. A feeling of nausea swept over him as he contemplated the implications of his action. This was an existential nausea, caused by his intense awareness of the contingency of life, and could not be relieved with an ordinary Alka-Seltzer. What was required was an Existential Alka-Seltzer – a product sold in many Left Bank drugstores. It was an enormous pill, the size of an automobile hubcap, that, dissolved in water, took away the queasy feeling induced by too much awareness of life. Cloquet had also found it helpful after eating Mexican food.

Granted, Allen's humor depends on parody – in this case, of Sartre, of Camus – for its energy, but he is also not above poking fun at those would-be intellectuals who take such writers and their philosophies "seriously." I belabor these matters partly because Allen belabors them, and partly because I was struck recently by the painstaking rigor a scholar has brought to bear on Mark Twain's reading habits. Apparently, this professor has assembled enough evidence to prove what every serious reader of Twain already knew – namely, that Twain owned, and read, and, yes, *underlined*, large numbers of books, and that he perpetrated the mythos of the rustic, homespun spinner of tall tales and dispenser of lowfalutin wisdom so as not to put off any segment of the population with the ready cash to buy one of his books or to crowd into one of his lectures. (Maybe this scholar's next effort, with similarly important results, will be to demonstrate the opposite about Woody Allen – namely, that he reads dust jackets and reviews, rather than real books, and that he perpetrates the mythos of a sensitive New York egghead so he will remain the darling of those who also make it a point to keep up with our culture by reading the *New York Review of Books.*)

Perhaps for the same reasons as those attributed to Mark Twain, Benchley wrote his considerable learning lightly – whether he was delivering Harvard's Ivy Day Oration, reviewing plays for the *New Yorker*, or assuming the Joe Doakesian mantle as America's beleaguered Common Man. In contrast, Allen has insisted both on remaining Allen and, as the title of his first collection suggests, on *Getting Even.* Compare, for example, the "concept" lurking behind Benchley's Ivy Day Oration with Allen's "My Speech to the Graduates." Like the befuddled "treasurer" who must give his report – indeed, like a host of his other personae who arrive breathless and more than a little overwhelmed – Benchley's student speaker is surprised "at being just now suddenly called upon to address you":

> . . . here it was Class Day, and there I was in my room hemming napkins. Quickly I drew on a pair of shoes and my cap and gown, and breaking into a run – and a perspiration – soon found myself, unless I am mistaken, here.

Allen works with more pretentious rhetoric, and he knows how to give the clichés of June just the right satiric twist:

> More than any other time in history, mankind faces a crossroads. One path leads to despair and utter hopelessness. The other, to total extinction. Let us pray we have the wisdom to choose correctly.

But even Allen as a pompous graduation speaker cannot resist the temptation to sound like other Allen personae – that is, to yoke the wildly disparate via the absurd juxtaposition: "How is it possible to find meaning in a finite world given my waist and shirt size?"

Allen's career has been something of an odyssey, a humorist's search for congenial turf. In this regard, he and Benchley are kindred spirits, but with this important difference: Allen found in film what Benchley never imagined was there – namely, a chance to exploit his talents to their fullest, and to do this with integrity and independence. He has also been lucky enough to work at a time when filmmakers matter. Here, too, Allen plays to a hipper house.

| | |

Timing is, indeed, all – not only with regard to *how* the comic tale is told but also with regard to its cultural context: its *where* and *when* and with what technology. Benchley's finest achievements enjoyed their brief decades on the revue stage and then lingered in the memory of those fortunate enough to have seen them firsthand. To be sure, some films of Benchley in minor roles exist, but he is hardly served well when a high-water mark such as "The Treasurer's Report" grows ever dustier behind the Museum of Modern Art's imposing walls, preserved *from* the general public. In contrast, we (and future generations) can easily bring Allen's recordings and films to the scales of critical justice.

Yet it is important to realize that timing also affects critical assessments, and that only after fifty years or so will we be able to judge Allen's achievement as fully, as disinterestedly, as we are now prepared to judge Benchley's. In this sense, Benchley's reputation – as a consummate humorist in his own right, and as an abiding influence to succeeding generations of *New Yorker* writers – has been diminished by time but is still impressive. It remains to be seen whether or not the best of Woody Allen's *New Yorker* sketches (e.g., "The Metterling Lists," "Death Knocks," "Remembering Needleman," "My Apology," "The Kugelmass Episode," and "The Whore of Mensa") will survive as long.

If even half the accounts of Woody Allen's driving perfectionism are true, he has apparently made much of his luck, and I suspect that future critics will regard him as a case of Blakean persistence rewarded, of a person pursuing his neuroses until they become the very stuff of art. But even here, cultural timing will play a significant role, for humor is a fragile commodity and public taste is notoriously fickle. What was sooooo funny one year is not necessarily funny a decade later. Mark Twain once speculated about why humorists such as Artemus Ward and Josh Billings, Orpheus C. Kerr, and Smith O'Brien – all popular in their day – had faded from the collective memory, and he concluded that they were merely funny: "A humorist must not professedly preach and he must not professedly teach, but he must do both if he would live forever." Twain, I should add, then went on to define "forever" as thirty years. By such a reckoning, Woody Allen has been an important fixture on the American scene – as a gag writer and stand-up comic, as a writer for the *New Yorker*, and as a filmmaker – for longer than "forever." I take that as a good sign of America's long-standing love affair with first-rate humor, and as a good portent for its future.

Lenny Bruce:
Shpritzing the *Goyim* /
Shocking the Jews

Now I neologize Jewish and goyish.
Dig: I'm Jewish. Count Basie's Jewish.
Ray Charles is Jewish. Eddie Cantor's
goyish. *B'nai Brith is* goyish;
Hadassah, Jewish. Marine corps –
heavy goyish, *dangerous. Koolaid is*
goyish. *All Drake's Cakes are* goyish.
Pumpernickel is Jewish, and, as
you know, white bread is very
goyish. . . . *Black cherry soda's very*
Jewish. Macaroons are very
Jewish – very Jewish cake. Fruit salad
is Jewish. Lime jello is goyish. *Lime*
soda is very goyish.
from *The Essential Lenny Bruce*

T he words of a dead man," W. H. Auden tells us, "are
modified in the guts of the living." He had a fellow-poet,
William Butler Yeats, in mind, but the sentiment holds
true as well for Lenny Bruce. For some time now we have
been modifying (or, to use a fancier term, transmogrifying) Lenny
Bruce, reimagining him – on stage, on screen, in biographies and
critical articles – as prophet, as guru, as rabbi, as satirist, as
stand-up comic, but, most of all, as martyr.

Let me begin by considering him as neologist, a word he used
shamelessly and without credentials, but which suggests something

of the cultural landscape he both came from and forever changed.
A neologist either invents new words or discovers new meanings for
old ones. Lenny Bruce did neither. He did not invent the word
shpritz, although he was no doubt its most important popularizer;
nor was he quite the innovator, the daring linguistic pioneer, that
the term neologist implies. But *words* were what mattered to him,
especially if they could take on the improvisational energy of a
Charlie Parker or the go-for-broke abandon of the streetcorner wise-
cracker. Words, showers of them, unleashed, sprayed, machine-
gunned at the audience until they "cracked up," couldn't *stand* it
anymore . . . that was Lenny Bruce's brand of neology whether he
was "working a room" or talking on the telephone.

Here, for example, is Bruce *shpritzing* the *goyim* in one of
his most famous bits – Religions Incorporated. The scene is the
headquarters where the movers-and-shakers (Oral Roberts, Billy
Graham, Patamunzo Yogananda, Danny Thomas, Eddie Cantor,
Pat O'Brien, General Sarnoff, and others) are conducting some
heavy business. Bruce begins in parody – in this case, the syrupy
southern voice of H. A. Allen – but he ends in pure *shpritz*, a tor-
rent of images and off-the-wall associations:

> Now, gentlemen, we got mistuh Necktyuh, from our reli-
> gious novelty house in Chicago, who's got a beautiful sel-
> luh – the gen-yew-ine Jewish-star-lucky-cross-cigarette-
> lighter combined; an we got the kiss-me-in-the-dahk
> *mezzuzah*; an the wawk-me-tawk-me camel; an these wunner-
> ful lil cocktail napkins with some helluva saying theah –
> "Anuthuh mahtini faw Muthuh Cabrini" – an some pretty far
> out things. . . .

Bruce was hardly the first satirist to equate hucksterism with piety,
to point out the dollar signs in officially God-fearing eyes, but
he was probably the first comic to turn these observations into
shtick. Of politics, there had been humor aplenty; about religion –
especially the sort that named names and imagined Mother Cabrini
cocktail napkins – there had been a conspicuous vacuum before
Lenny Bruce. His *shpritz* turned organized religion into a big,
Spencer Gifts business.

If scat singers like Ella Fitzgerald or Mel Torme can turn the human voice into a wailing saxophone or a screeching trumpet, Bruce's *shpritz* used words as if they were drumsticks: *bam – bam – bam*. The result was a rapid-fire rhythm that broke the rules of timing older comics like George Burns and Jack Benny had lived by, but Bruce's manic energy, his relentless pounding, also "broke up" the crowd.

To be sure, *shtetl* humorists were also "verbal," but with some important differences. They "unpacked their hearts" within the religious, cultural, and socio-political frameworks of the Jewish community, giving vent in *words* to frustrations that often arrived with the sanction of law or at the end of a gentile fist. Reviewing Sholom Aleichem's *Motl the Cantor's Son*, Saul Bellow put it this way:

Powerlessness appears to force people to have recourse to words. Hamlet has to unpack his heart with words, he complains. The fact that the Jews of Eastern Europe lived among menacing and powerful neighbors no doubt contributed to the subtlety and richness of the words with which they unpacked.

By contrast, subtlety was hardly Bruce's strong suit. His *shpritz* was designed to overwhelm, overpower, overkill. It thrived on confrontation, on making painfully public what *shtetl* humorists thought and said privately, with caution and, of course, in Yiddish.

That is why Bruce, for all the Yiddishisms he peppered through his monologues, bears but a slight resemblance to the traditions of Yiddish humor. He is too brassy, too cocksure of himself, finally too *American*. He learned the fine points of *shpritzing* not from Mendele Mocher Seforim or Sholom Aleichem (writers one has every reason to suspect he never read or, for that matter, knew about), but, rather, from a legendary character named Joe Ancis. As Albert Goldman's biography-as-*shpritz/shpritz*-as-biography would have it, Bruce met Ancis, the Ur-sick-comic, at Hanson's, a hangout for comics that doubled as a drugstore/luncheonette. In 1947, a quarter would buy an egg cream and all the shtick, the patter, and talk about the business that a down-on-his-heels comic could want. If New Orleans gave birth to the blues, Hanson's is where *shpritz* first went semiprofessional. Ancis eyeballed Bruce and decided to

give him the Jewish version of what Blacks call "playing the dozens." He pinned a young woman against the counter and, in Goldman's reconstruction of those times, that place, neologized her as
follows:

> "Oi, is this a fucking grape-jelly job! Varicosities on the legs.
> Sweat stains under the arms. Cotton panties from Kresge's
> with the days of the week. Always wears the wrong day. Schleps
> home to Carnarsie every night. Her old man beats her up
> while the mother listens to the radio in a wheelchair. Supper
> is ham and eggs and grits and all that Southern-dummy-
> cheapo-drecky-dumbbell shit."

Ancis cracked the joint up – with enough pure cataloging to make
Walt Whitman envious, but, unlike the sonorous bard, delivered
with a manic energy that always seemed on the edge of going completely out of control . . . and yet never quite did. In short, Ancis
was the consummate *shpritzer*, an artist who had enough hidden
verbal reserves to outlast even the toughest competition.

What Ancis lacked, however, was the raw courage or, if you
will, the chutzpah necessary to work as a professional stand-up
comic. *That*, as it turned out, Lenny Bruce had in abundance. He
was a Brooklyn version of the frontier braggart who could reel off
outrageous claims faster than his listeners could either digest them
or register their dissent.

In a word, Bruce *overwhelmed* his audiences. But, unlike the
ring-tailed roarers so dear to the heart of southwestern humorists,
Bruce was more prone to direct his scathing commentary "outward." At the same time, ironically enough, he was perhaps the
first Jewish stand-up comic to make regular raids on his autobiography. Instead of appropriating, and appealing to, the insular life
of the Jewish community (as Yiddish humorists from Mendele
Mocher Seforim to the Borscht Belt vaudevillians had, in effect,
done), Bruce turned stage-center into a forum for free associating
about the *goyim* and the Jews. The result coarsened Jewish material. At the same time he sharpened its public sting. When Bruce
insists, for example, that "Pumpernickel is Jewish and, as you
know, white bread is very *goyish*," he both reduces "difference" to

a matter of supermarket preference and makes it clear that the Jews were hipper, smarter, superior, *chosen* – because they saw their corned beef through a rye, darkly. At the same time, when Bruce explains that his irreverence results from having "no knowledge of the [Jewish] god . . . because to have a god you have to know something about him, and as a child I couldn't speak the same language as the Jewish god," the ignorance he glibly equates with alienation may well be the central truth of American-Jewish assimilation. If these quotations smack of contradiction, Bruce, like Whitman, did not especially worry: "So I contradicted myself," I can hear his ghost *shreiing*, "so what?" He, too, contained multitudes – in this case, the popular culture he absorbed half by osmosis, half by catch-up reading; the American-Jewish culture he regarded as albatross and badge of honor; the hipster ethos he lived, and died, for.

Irving Howe, clearly as admiring as he is embarrassed by Bruce's mean-spirited, unrelentingly public attacks on *Yiddishkleit* describes the Bruce phenomenon this way:

> Humor of this kind bears a heavy weight of destruction; in Jewish hands, more likely self-destruction, for it proceeds from a brilliance that corrodes the world faster than, even in imagination, it can remake it. A corrupt ascetic is a man undone. Bruce remained a creature of show biz, addicted to values he despised, complicit at the "upper" levels of his life in the corruption of the big time and yielding at the "lower" levels to the lure of drugs and chaos.

Mordecai Richler, the comic novelist, puts the matter more bluntly: "Lenny Bruce did not die for my sins."

To *shpritz* the *goyim*/to shock the Jews – that is to describe what Bruce did, rather than to turn his self-styled neology into a modern jeremiad, his neuroses into the stuff of martyrdom. If Mort Sahl used the evening newspaper as a source for "material," as a prop for his comic timing and as a way of juxtaposing liberal (Jewish?) values against American hypocrisy, Bruce often resorted to that last refuge of the freshman essay – definition, according to Webster:

Now, a Jew, in the dictionary, is one who is descended from the ancient tribes of Judea, or one who is regarded as descended from that tribe.

That, of course, is the definition, but the culture knows better and, moreover, it operates – just below the surface of polite, liberal pieties – on what it *knows*. As Bruce puts it, with a matter-of-factness that usually preceded his more trenchant observations: "but you and I know what a Jew is – *One Who Killed Our Lord*." Long before blowing the whistle on this-or-that conspiracy, on this-or-that official cover-up, Bruce used the *emmis*, the truth, to pack them in at the hipper houses:

> Alright, I'll clear the air once and for all, and confess. Yes, I did it, my family. I found a note in my basement. It said: "We killed him. Signed, Morty."

An older generation of Catskill comics – who did material of the Jews, for the Jews and, most important of all, *in* "Jewish" – knew instinctively that some things were tasteless, *schmutzike* ("dirty"), not funny – even at Grossinger's. But in front of "mixed" crowds like those at nightclubs like the "hungry i"? Unthinkable! There was simply too much history, too much felt pain, packed into their immigrant bones, much less into the more conventional bones of their audiences. Besides, if Bruce could shock such Jews by aping the affected talk of reform rabbis ("Today, on Chin-ukka, with Rose-o-shonah approaching . . .") and letting us in on the "truth" about God (rabbi: "What cheek! To ask [if God exists or not] in a temple! We're not here to talk of God – we're here to sell bonds for Israel!"), he could also misfire rather badly: "A *mezzuzah* is a Jewish chapstick. That's why they're always kissing it when they go out." The first examples are the stuff of satire and, of course, the occasion for predictable charges about self-hatred; on the other hand, the wisecrack about chapstick *mezzuzahs* falls flat, embarrassing in its ignorance and sheer pointlessness.

Bruce, of course, put as much distance as he could between himself and the conventional, the timid, the fainthearted. His appeal was a willingness – indeed, a compulsion – to tell the *emmis* (the truth) as it was, and still is. "Maybe it would shock some people," Bruce insisted, moving toward the sermon that often replaced the punch line of conventional comics, "to say that we killed him at his own request, because he knew that people would exploit him. . . . In Christ's name they would exploit the flag, the Bible, and – *whew!* Boy, the things they've done in his name."

His riff on Blacks that began "By the way, are there any niggers here tonight?" shows that Bruce understood that language is power, and also that the words that hurt can be words defused, exhausted by repetition (e.g., "That's two kikes, and three niggers," Bruce would begin, in the guise of a Southern tobacco auctioneer, "and one spic. One spic – two, three spics, One mick. One mick, one spic, one hick, thick, funky, spunky boogie. . . .") The point, of course, is that

> if President Kennedy got on television and said, "Tonight I'd like to introduce the niggers in my cabinet," and he yelled "niggerniggerniggerniggernigger" at every nigger he saw and "boogeyboogeyboogey, niggerniggernigger" 'till nigger lost its meaning – you'd never make any four-year-old nigger cry when he came home from school.

Litany, then, became for Bruce a species of exorcism, a way to purify the language by purgation.

The rub, of course, is that there was more to Bruce's modus operandi than "shock" and certainly much, much more than labels like "sick comic" could cover. For the hipster, the world divided (a bit too neatly) into the "with-it's" and the squares, into those who dug *real* jazz (Charlie Parker) and those who bought Montavani records. Those "in-between," as it were, wore madras shirts and belt-in-the-back pants, owned all the Brubeck albums, thought of themselves both as liberal and as majoring in the liberal-arts. They swelled the crowd on weekends and, not surprisingly, a high percentage of these medium-rollers were Jewish.

For them, Bruce was a clean break from the tedious, predictable patter of the Borscht Belt comics their parents still found funny. This guy could really do a number on bigots, on religious hypo-

crites, on the smug complacencies of a smug, majority culture. To
walk out complaining that Bruce was a "toilet mouth," that "enough-
was-enough" was to put yourself on record as the enemy. To laugh,
to clap approvingly or, better yet, to simply nod and let out a soul-
ful "yeaaaa" was to be on the side of the left-thinking angels.

Shtick about Nazis became the acid test. Long before Mel Brooks
gave us the outrageous production number from *The Producers*
called "Springtime for Hitler," Bruce had thrown this bit of off-the-
cuff analysis at his audiences:

> Eichmann really figured, you know, "The Jews – the most
> liberal people in the world – they'll give me a fair shake."
> Fair? *Certainly.* "Rabbi" means lawyer. He'll get the best trial
> in the world. Eichmann. *Ha!* They were shaving his leg while
> he was giving his appeal! That's the last bit of insanity, man.

It was, of course, easy to sit through Bruce's put-downs of middle
America, with its small towns ("You go to the park, see the cannon,
and you've had it.") and small minds (working a Milwaukee club,
Bruce figures "these are the *Grey Line tourers*, before they leave!
This is where they *live.*"), but send-ups about the Holocaust were
more than the over-thirty Jewish crowd could take. What he said
about Eichman was not only "tasteless," it was forbidden, taboo,
altogether unacceptable.

To be sure, Bruce, being Bruce, was never at a loss for words,
especially for those words which explained, which rationalized,
which put whatever he said under the large protective covering
called "satire":

> But here's the thing on comedy. If I were to do a satire on
> the assassination of John Foster Dulles, it would shock people.
> They'd say, "That is in heinous taste." Why? Because it's
> fresh. And that's why my contention is: that satire is tragedy
> plus time. You give it enough time, the public, the reviewers
> will allow you to satirize it. Which is rather ridiculous when
> you think about it. And I know, probably 500 years from to-
> day, someone will do a satire on Adolf Hitler, maybe even

showing him as a hero, and everyone will laugh. . . . And yet
if you did it today, it would be bad.

What Bruce didn't figure on, however, was the distinction between a satirical sketch about John Foster Dulles's assassination –
where terms like "tasteless" and "sick" were sure to follow – and
shtick about Hitler that raised the issue of self-hatred. Consider,
for example, Bruce's "fantasy" about Hitler's "discovery" by a
quasi-Jewish, fast-talking talent agent ("I like dot first name –
Adolf – it's sort ov off beat. I like that."). But *Shicklegruber*? A last
name like that will never do:

> Ve need something to, sort of, hit people. . . . Adolf Hit –
> No. Adolf Hit-ler – zat's a vild name, right? A-d-o-l-f H-i-t-l-e-r.
> Five and six for the marquee – nice and zmall. Dot's nice.
> Dot's right. Ve get a little rhythm section behind him, it'll
> sving dere. Jonah Jones, maybe.

Bruce, of course, knew about pseudonyms first-hand, having come
into the world as Leonard Alfred Schneider. Lenny Bruce – with its
back-to-back first names and requisite number of spaces for the
marquee – was a monicker with snap to it – quick, no-nonsense
and, best of all, not stuck in the immigrant world of exhausted,
defeated Schneiders. Like the Great Gatsby – who metamorphosed
himself from his unlikely, humble origins as Jay Gatz – Bruce
"sprang from his Platonic conception of himself." The difference,
of course, is that while Gatsby's forward motion is fueled by a deep,
unquestioning belief in the American Dreams that ultimately destroyed him, it was the subculture that kept Bruce hopping. He
took corrosion, rather than innocence, as his special province and,
as such, his manic energy had a decidedly Manichean edge. The
Princes of Good and Evil warred within his best material, as "defi-
nitions" of each – what Bruce liked to call the *emmis* – did acro-
batic leaps across the conjunction.

In short, he was out to exorcize whatever impulses toward Jewishness, toward "restraint" still clung to his bones. If an immigrant
generation believed that God gave us bodies so that our heads

wouldn't fall off, if the observant wore *gartels* (sashes) to divide the higher portions (the holier) from the lower (the profane), Bruce was out to liberate – yea, to celebrate – the fleshly:

> Now, lemme hip you to something. Lemme tell you something. If you believe that there is a god, a god that made your body, and yet you think you can do anything with that body that's dirty, then the fault lies with the manufacturer. *Emmis.*

For Bruce, *emmis* is akin to *selah*, to *omayn*. In philosophical argument, it would be represented *quod erat demonstrandum* ("which was to be demonstrated"). Either way, Bruce hath spoken and matters of the body need not detain us any longer.

Bruce's wide-openness encompassed more than the mouth and the genitals – what one said and, sexually speaking, whatever one chose to do. It also included, in increasing doses, whatever one could smoke or swallow or shoot-up. The body's excitement, rather than Jewish fearfulness, was alone worth exploring, worth the Faustian challenge. What Alexander Portnoy *kvetches* about in *Portnoy's Complaint*, Philip Roth's testament to American-Jewish emancipation ("The guilt, the fears – the terror bred into my bones! What in their world was not charged with danger, dripping with germs, fraught with peril?"), Bruce turned into shock, into *shpritz* and into what, in California, is called a lifestyle:

> I think that a lot of marriages went West, you know, they split up, in my generation, because ladies didn't know that guys were different . . . to a lady [cheating] means kissing hugging and liking somebody. You have to at least *like* somebody. With guys that doesn't enter into it. . . . Like, a lady can't go through a plate glass window and go to bed with you five seconds later. But every guy in this audience is the same – you can *idolize* your wife, just be so crazy about her, be on the way home from work, have a head-on collision with a Greyhound bus, in a *disaster* area. Forty people laying dead on the highway – not even in the hospital, in the *ambulance* – the guy makes a play for the nurse.

It's very possible that —— —— is *very* sexual. He's just probably a very horny cat – makes it with guys, chicks, mud, sheep, anything: his fist. He's a real *haisser* – that could be, couldn't it?

Like all of us: me, you, you, you – put us on a desert island for five years, no chicks, you'll ball mud. *Emmis.* You *have*, man. *Knotholes.*

Moreover, his view from the sleazy underbelly of show biz credentialled the *emmis* of what he said, in roughly the same way that the "cult of experience" had authenticated people like Stephen Crane or John Steinbeck or Ernest Hemingway. "Bruce was *there*, man. He had *seen* it" – which, for twenty-year-old college students is, presumably, all that needs to be said.

The trouble with confusing so much patter with so much "truth," of course, is that Bruce's monologues are to the hip what Kahlil Gibran's *The Prophet* is to the square. Pearl K. Bell once wrote a shrewd review with the intriguing title "Philip Roth: Sonny Boy or Lenny Bruce." In it, she says this of the Roth who provided David Kepesh, *The Professor of Desire*, with the temper tantrums we recognize as vintage Roth:

> Roth seems to believe that the only two choices of being available to a grown Jewish man are Al Jolson's sonny boy or Lenny Bruce. In fact, the erudite professor sounds oddly like soap opera, where people fall in and out of love as though life were a swimming pool (so life is *not* like a swimming pool).

To be sure, Roth is a sit-down comedian, a writer, whose "influences," anxiety-producing or otherwise, are more likely to be Kafka or Gogol or Chekov, rather than a Lenny Bruce. Besides, Bruce shed early whatever persona might have separated him from Leonard Alfred Schneider. His "act," as it were, was his life. Roth has always insisted – usually without much success – that he is not Neil Klugman, not Alexander Portnoy, not Nathan Zuckerman.

What the two culture heroes have in common, however, is a wide streak of the Puritanical, albeit turned upside-down. Roth, apparently, would like nothing better than to add Jewish protagonists who do the unthinkable – that is, run wild, unbridled, restlessly unsatisfied – to the official canon of tame "Jewish books." But the enterprise has a desperate ring about it, as if Roth were trying too hard to be morally liberated. Bruce, on the other hand, insisted on having his self-righteous cake at the same time he *shtupped* it into his mouth. Guilt was, presumably, other people's hang-up, yet Bruce's flights into hedonism (usually by way of various "fantasies") had a way of being coupled with "instruction." His aphorisms, his epigrammatic wit, slipped easily – perhaps *too* easily – into large pronouncements:

> If I could just rob fifty words out of your head I could stop the war. . . .

> The reason I got busted – arrested – is I picked on the wrong god.

> My concept? You can't do *anything* with anybody's body to make it dirty to me. Six people, eight people, one person – you can do only one thing to make it dirty: kill it. Hiroshima was dirty. Chessman was dirty.

That *Playboy* magazine found this "good copy" is hardly surprising. Everything conventionally thought and said about the 1950s suggests that repression was long overdue for the gospel according to Hefner. The Playboy "Bunny" was, in this sense, a stroke of (advertising) genius that, for far too many, became associated with genius per se. The magazine published long excerpts from Bruce's autobiographical romp, *How to Talk Dirty and Influence People*, and a seemingly endless mish-mash of the liberal and the hedonistic called "The Playboy Philosophy." Bruce, the entertainer, was in danger of being taken seriously as Bruce, the prophet, as Bruce, the discerning social commentator. Even more important, Bruce was in danger of taking *himself* seriously, of becoming that saddest of all tricksters – the con man conned. In this respect, Buddy Hackett – yet another pioneer in the popularization of "dirty words" and blunt, tasteless talk – has fared better. Partly because he is roly-poly, partly because his physical brand of clowning exudes little boyishness, Hackett stands outside the pale of censorship. He is, in a word, funny – rather than "one of us."

At the end, of course, Bruce found himself cast in the role of defendant, pleading his case to audiences that had come to see his old bits: "Religions Incorporated," "The Lone Ranger," "Father Flotsky," "Tits-'N-Ass." Instead, their cover charge bought them readings from the transcripts of his trials and his anguished, Joseph K-ish responsa. Those with a fascination for the stuff of legend, who understood that, in America, nothing succeeds like failure, sat transfixed through Bruce's harrowing: others, expecting yuks, shot the ragged-out, black-suited *maggid* (preacher) a sour look and headed toward the exits. The Bruce who had *shpritzed* the *goyim*, who had shocked the Jews, ended by boring both.

Since Bruce overdosed during the long, hot summer of 1966, other casualties have followed in his footsteps, most notably Freddie Prinze of "Chico and the Man" fame and John Belushi, the resident wild-man of "Saturday Night Live." With these cases, videotape provides a performance record that can be judged dispassionately, when the "sympathy vote" is finally in. For better or worse, Bruce's best work was live. There are record albums, of course, and a few attempts to catch his act on film, but the overall effect is rather like trying to judge a legendary tenor like Caruso from a scratchy 78. Moreover, Bruce on the printed page is hardly Bruce at his finest. The material not dated by its references to that time, those places, has a stilted, sophomoric ring if read aloud today. What it lacks is Bruce's timing, his gestures, his pauses, even his nervous "you know's."

Nonetheless, Bruce continues to matter – not only to those true believers who would insist that Lenny Bruce was "murdered" because he told the truth or to those who would place his ideas ahead of William James's or Alfred North Whitehead's, but also to those more modest souls who see Bruce in the context of what he was, what he did and what he made possible. A stand-up comic like George Carlin, for example, continues Bruce's satiric investigations into our language – the words we forbid as well as those we use without thinking. Troupes like "Second City" (best known in their incarnations on "SCTV") continue the parodic romps through our popular culture that Bruce pioneered without elaborate props or the aid-and-comfort of repertory players. In a word, Bruce made stand-up comedy as it is currently being practiced at clubs like "Catch a Rising Star" or the "Comedy Store" possible. Granted, he did not create our permissive, no-holds-barred environment single-handedly (the cunning of history, especially as the Vietnam War divided our country into culture versus counterculture, can lay greater claim to this dubious benefit), but it is fair to say that he paid dues – heavy dues – early.

And yet, after we have laid our obligatory wreath on Bruce's tomb and pointed to those aspects of his career that were unique and important, there are continuities worth mentioning. If Bruce was a phenomenon that only the 1950s could have created and only the 1960s could have loved, he was also some very old Manische-witz wrapped inside a new brown paper bag. The urban vaudeville comic knew that American humor put its emphasis on the adjective, that ethnic stereotyping (e.g., the drunken Irishman, the shuffling African-American, and money-hungry Jew) was always good for a laugh.

For turn-of-the-century Jewish comics, the traditions of American humor meant that charm gave way to meanness. Take, for example, two representative "fire stories," the first firmly within the Yiddish tradition:

> A Jew pays a call on the rabbi of a small community and tells him a heartbreaking story. He has been the victim of a terrible fire, one that destroyed his house and everything he owned. In short, he has been reduced to penury and now he travels from town to town collecting what charity he can. "Can you help me, rabbi?" the poor man asks.
>
> "And have you a document from the rabbi of your town testifying that you are, indeed, a fire victim?" the suspicious rabbi inquires.
>
> "Absolutely. Without question," the man replies, "but, unfortunately, it too was burnt."

Granted, the victim/beggar's "deception" is paper-thin, but the wit, the *fiction*, if you will, makes measures of dignity possible both for the giver and the receiver of help. The question, in short, is not Who was hurt by the ruse? but rather, How can even a joke speak for people? The alternative, after all, is *charity* — that which often leads to self-righteousness in the do-gooder and a robbed humanity in the done-to.

By contrast, here is how East Broadway turned the typical "fire story" into its sleazy American cousin:

> One Jew meets another on the street and says: "So, Abe, I hear you had a fire in your store last week."
>
> "Quiet, quiet," Abe replies, "it's *next* week."

Granted, vaudeville humor had a rough edge — evidently one with staying power, if the sales figures for *Truly Tasteless Jokes* are any indication — but the hidden agenda just behind the cheap laughs was clear: shed your ethnic differences, assimilate into mainstream America, in a word, melt. When an Abie meets an Ike, what they invariably talk about is how they cheated the *goyim* — by torching a store, by swapping the goods, or by simply overcharging. These stage Jews were smart all right, but they were also unethical, unsavory, just plain greedy. Who did *they* hurt? This time the answer was clear: America, which is to say, the *goyim*.

Bruce knew the tradition, and he insisted that it was "cruel":

> The comedy they had *before*, I think, actually was cruel. . . . There was the Jew comic, they used to call them; the Wop comic, they used to say; they used to do the blackface, real stereotype Uncle Tom Jim Crow with the curls and fright wig. . . . I think the comedy of today has more of a liberal viewpoint.

Bruce, of course, began with stereotypes and then went on to give them the send-up, the *shpritz* they deserved. His Blacks insist, for example, that "the furst ting I gwine do when I gwine get to Hebbin is fine out what a 'gwine' is." But without Blacks, without Catholics, without homosexuals and, to be sure, without Jews, Bruce had no act.

To be sure, Bruce's comedy was light-years beyond the predictability of easy punch lines and socko finishes. In the lingo of exasperated agents, Bruce "played to the band" – meaning that he *shpritzed* a good many curve balls that conventional audiences simply didn't catch. But, at bottom, his were differences of degree rather than of kind. He went after those with identifiable religious affiliations not only because he found them hypocritical, but because, for him, liberalism was religion enough; he went after the middle-class not only because they were smug, but because they weren't hipsters; he went after southerners not only because they were racists, but because any regionalisms (outside New York City) were suspect. In short, Bruce imagined a tea-colored, compassionate America, one that would swing and that would not hassle people if they talked dirty or smoked a little dope. Best of all, Bruce imagined that this better America would be neither Jewish nor *goyish*. And like most people who dwell on the "big picture," Bruce preferred to think that God was made in *his* image, rather than the other way around:

> He's any kind of god you want him to be, god, that's what he is . . . he's a pumpkin god, he's a halloween god, he's a good sweet loving god who'll make me burn in hell for my sins and blaspheming, he's that kind of god, too. . . . And he's a god that you can exploit and make work for you, and get you respect in the community, and get St. Jude working for you, and all those other Catholic priests, Jewish – Eddie Cantor, putz-o exploiter, George E. Jessel and Kiss-it-off Santas. Yeah, he's a god that'll look at this culture and say, "*Whew!* What were they *doing*, man? They've got people in prison for thirty-five years!"

Not surprisingly, this last "god" – the hip one, with a social conscience – sounds like a dead ringer for Lenny Bruce.

What shocked in Bruce was his unrelenting attack on the values Jews and non-Jews alike had melted into – the pieties of organized religion, the conventions of heterosexual marriage, the world according to *Time* magazine. His *shpritz* was the word-as-weapon, the "free association" (often freer than it was associative) that played over everything – the autobiographical, the socio-cultural, the sacred and the profane — without compromising, or believing any of it.

Only Bruce could tell an audience that he was "going to piss on you" ("You can't photograph it — it's like rain") or ask for a big hand as he "introduced" Adolf Hitler. He may have squirmed under the label of "vomic" or felt that a word like "sick" belonged to the culture at large rather than to him, but outrage buttered his bread and bought his dope.

Among his more reflective moments, this one may be the most permanently revealing:

> Today's comedian has a cross to bear that he built himself. A comedian of the older generation did an "act" and he told the audience, "This is my act." Today's comic is not doing an act. The audience assumes he's telling the truth. . . . [And] when I'm interested in a truth, it's really a *truth* truth, one hundred per cent. And that's a terrible truth to be interested in.

For Bruce, the need to shock the Jews, to go public with their secrets, the need to *shpritz* the *goyim*, to exorcize all their "Southern-dummy — cheapo-drecky — dumbbell shit," all their white bread Protestantism, raised comedy-as-hostility and comedy-as-tragic catharsis to new levels, and to new expectations. Since Bruce's untimely exit, put-downs of mass culture have hardened into formula (the rise-and-fall of "Saturday Night Live," for example), and professional defenders of the Jewish faith have had Philip Roth's continuing efforts to kick around. But Bruce got to the sensitive nerves first, and in ways that can still *shpritz* the *goyim* into helpless laughter and shock the Jews into uncomfortable worry. As Bruce once put it, "All my humor is based upon destruction and despair." A good deal of the "destruction and despair" came from, and was restricted to, Bruce's life; but sizable portions were, and continue to be, part of ours as well.

Some Faces of Cultural Politics

To argue that literature does not exist in a vacuum is simultaneously to express a truth and to ask for trouble. For cultural politics is the testy, contentious crossroads where literature and ideology often clash. In this sense, there is nothing indeterminate about what some regard as our indeterminate age; those who bring special interests and specific cultural agendas to their readings of literature know better. To the victors go the ideological spoils: national magazines in which kindred spirits can skewer the opposition, the rest-and-recreation offered up by well-heeled think tanks and foundations, and the sense (real or imagined) of political influence.

"Bashing the Liberals: How the Neoconservatives Make Their Point" takes a hard look at one aspect of the phenomenon – namely, at those who have made revisionism their watchword. In this sense, presidential elections are not the only place where old-fashioned liberals are likely to find themselves being abused; neoconservative attacks against the Left – both Old and New – are now regularly launched by those who write for magazines such as *Commentary* or the *New Criterion*. The bad news is not that their political squabbling is so heated, so polemical, so often mean-spirited (when, one could argue, was it otherwise?), but rather that the spirit of revisionism they embody threatens to turn literary study itself into an armed ideological camp.

Small wonder that many declare the contest a draw and retreat to their studies to write about subjects arcane, circumscribed, and, most important of all, uncontroversial. Meanwhile, the assaults against literature and the humane spirit – from the ideological Right as well as the fanatical Left – continue.

At the same time, however, to take the moral consequences of intellectual work seriously is to raise fundamental questions about metaphor and, by extension, about literary study itself. The current debate about Paul de Man which crackled through the pages of everything from *Time* to *Critical Inquiry* – and which serves as the major focus of "Modernist Culture, the Cunning of History, and Paul de Man" – provides one such occasion. Admittedly the issue is as complicated as the implications are shivery. But there are at least six million reasons why de Man must be held accountable. Perhaps the best one can do at this point is provide a historical overview of those elements of modernism that led to the gas chambers, and to see de Man's wartime complicity as inextricably linked to his later evasiveness and to the nihilism of his literary philosophy. This, however, represents a beginning – and yet another instance of the bad news that responsible critics must bear.

The section ends, however, on quite another note, one designed to be simultaneously celebratory and instructive. "Lost Causes/ Marginal Hopes: The Collected Elegies of Irving Howe" provides a restrospective account of Howe's career as an activist and social critic. As such it is a portrait of a man of letters who not only bore much of the bad news recounted in the first two essays, but also managed to stay a steady course on behalf of what is best in our literature and in ourselves.

Bashing the Liberals:
How the Neoconservatives
Make Their Point

I n an effort to make clear sense of the plethora of books being published about the New York intellectuals, Hilton Kramer, editor of the *New Criterion*, turns to Alexander Bloom's *Prodigal Sons: The New York Intellectuals and Their World* (1986) as an instructive case in point. Bloom, who teaches history at Wheaton College, is neither a scoundrel nor "your garden-variety left-wing militant." If he were, Kramer would, not doubt, have rolled out his big, neoconservative guns. But Bloom is worse, much worse, and so he falls into a category somewhere beneath contempt:

> What he is, in other words, is your quintessential liberal academic. He is not given to billboarding his Sixties ideology; he simply assumes, without argument and as a matter of course, that it is from the perspective of the Sixties that the history of the New York intellectuals must now be written. In this assumption he is entirely representative of his academic generation, and it is as a product of the regnant liberal academy – rather than as an account of its subject – that his book makes its principal claim on our attention.

If Kramer's impatience with yet another study of the *Partisan Review* crowd were merely a matter of pitting those who had been there against those who got it secondhand, and in their college's library stacks, one could dismiss the backbiting as unimportant. After all, polemics was never designed for the faint of heart, and Bloom must surely have known that he was grabbing hold of a hot wire when he set out to write a book about the likes of Lillian

Hellman and Mary McCarthy, Lionel Trilling and Philip Rahv. But Kramer is out to do more – much more – than merely excoriate Bloom for what he takes to be a dumb book. The barely disguised agenda in his piece is that "the history of the New York intellectuals – not the memoirs but the history – is being written from the perspective of the Left, with its touchstones of intellectual probity and achievement drawn from the 'idealism' of the Sixties and the political and cultural myths of the Thirties." Poor Bloom, had he put a wetter thumb to the political winds, had his history been more Right-thinking, he would, no doubt, have been the *New Criterion*'s academic hero rather than its goat.

I belabor the minor squirmish between Bloom's book and Kramer's review-essay because it strikes me as symptomatic of a wider cultural condition. No matter that terms like liberal and conservative, Right and Left, have become so slippery, so debased, that they are used almost exclusively for name-calling; no matter that one can name a dozen self-professed neoconservative essayists for every liberal who will stand and allow himself or herself to be counted; no matter that the doors of everything from think tanks to executive offices are open to what is popularly regarded as solid, down-to-earth, back-to-basics conservative thought – the plain fact is that bashing the liberals is what still gets the creative juices flowing.

Here, for example, is a representative section from Joseph Epstein's *Ambition* (1982), a book about the hopelessly naïve way our major American writers look at ambition, success, and money. What, Epstein asks, are the lessons that our best students learn when they take English 101, especially if their instructor has rumpled hair, a corduroy sports coat, drives a beat-up Volvo, and figures that the American Dream is so much bunk?

> Business, to begin with, is hypocritical and sterile (see *Babbitt*). Ambition is unseemly and everywhere suspect (see *What Makes Sammy Run*, *The Great Gatsby*, and, for nonreaders, the movies *Citizen Kane* and *The Apprenticeship of Duddy Kravitz*); middle-class life is essentially boring (see modern literature); upper-middle-class life, worse (see, these students

say, their own families). Affluence is a sham, a greedy affair bringing no happiness (see Galbraith et al.).

What is striking about Epstein's book is less its argument – there have always been those who felt that Mammon got the short end of High Art's stick, although the letters Ph.D. seldom followed their names – than its date of publication: 1980. Epstein teaches at fashionable Northwestern University, but one wonders how much time he spends on the campus, much less how much time he spends taking the contemporary student pulse. Granted, there was a time when students gave corporate recruiters the deaf ear – and often the bum's rush – but that was long ago and in what looks now like another country. The times, as the counterculture used to crow, are a-changin'. My guess is that Epstein's Northwestern – like my own college, indeed, like *any* institution in the higher education game – cannot hire business professors fast enough. Far from withering away for lack of ambition (Epstein's thesis), the truth is that today's students are shockingly candid about their greed.

But that much said, *Ambition* would have been wrongheaded even if it had appeared a decade earlier. Epstein's complaint is partly an exercise in keeping the 1960s alive so that he can kick it in the shins, partly an effort to show that academics can be as patriotic, as given to old-fashioned boosterism and pluck, as the next Rotarian. In fact, Epstein cannot quite resist "coming clean" about how he turned into a flag-waver:

One damp California morning, as I concluded a talk before the City Club of San Diego – there I am again, speaking to the rich – I was asked why my own ideas had begun to change. . . . I answered that I thought they had changed because I viewed the world as having changed. . . . Besides, I had a confession to make: once I dropped the belief that America was the foremost menace in the world, once I slipped free from the notion that further "programs" (more of the same, without any radical change in perspective or orientation) would alleviate domestic problems, I discovered that the United States, for all its faults, for all that still needed to be made better, was nonetheless a most impressive country – and I couldn't think of any other I should rather be living in. Now here is a startling confessional for an intellectual to make: I like it here.

Nothing quite beats candor as a strategy for grabbing the high ground. For confessional poets like Robert Lowell or Sylvia Plath, the shameful secrets they talked about had to do with divorce and alcoholism, suicidal impulses and madness. Here was a raw, undiluted poetry – and, best of all, one credentialed by actual lives, actual suffering. Epstein simply turns the art of confession on its head, not only by admitting that he likes it "here" – meaning America – but also that he likes it *here*, meaning the posh City Club of San Diego. Admittedly, he had once numbered himself among those who could give America the jeremiad it badly needed, but no longer. Why fight starched linen tablecloths, uniformed waiters, and five-course extravaganzas? Why bite the well-manicured hands so willing to feed him? After all, nobody likes a knocker. Besides, those *really* in the know – that is, the movers and shakers – know better. Your run-of-the-mill academic is not likely to know what fork to use, much less what to say at a lectern after lunch. The point of Epstein's sly "confession" is, of course, that *he* does.

Granted, one does not feel the full force of Epstein's agenda in a single essay. To read a collection like *Plausible Prejudices* (1985), however, is to see both pattern and perspective writ large. For Epstein, contemporary literature is firmly in the liberals' grip, and the result has been to foist no end of foolishness upon us:

> The invasion of politics into culture, in my view to an improper extent, has also helped to make literature in our day seem second-rate. Perhaps I am blinded by my own politics, but as I look about me I find that culture today in the United States is very much in thrall to political liberalism. The point is a bit complicated, but, as I view it, I find that, while the country is not particularly liberal, the culture has become increasingly so. If proof is wanted, I would point to the books that win prizes in the United States, to the politics of the men and women who constitute the majority of the membership of

the American Institute of Arts and Letters, to the critical and literary assumptions upon which so many contemporary American writers base their work.

Others have speculated about the widening gap between our cultural heroes and our culture, about the ever-thinning soup contemporary writers serve up and a mass readership increasingly convinced that literature no longer matters. Indeed, with the exception of those who have hitched their stars to post-postmodernist experimentation, nearly everybody else would agree that contemporary American literature is going through a bad patch. What makes Epstein's position distinctive, then, are not his smug satisfactions in calling naked emperors to our attention but, rather, his giddy delight in bashing the liberals who insist that American literature be a mirror turned to the Left:

> One poet who apparently draws unfailingly large crowds at universities is the feminist Adrienne Rich. I have never seen Miss Rich in performance. Doubtless hers is a fine enough show. Yet it does say something about the present state of literature that the only poet who can consistently draw large crowds at a university is a thoroughly politicized one. Universities have political agendas; they seem to want to do what they construe to be the right thing by all groups within the university community. Thus universities are quick – or at least they were quick, when the money was at hand – to set up black studies programs, women's studies programs, you name it. Because universities are disposed to this general view, literature under their auspices has come to look a little like the Democratic Party under George McGovern.

Epstein, of course, can vote with his feet whenever an unworthy Black writer or ideologically shrill feminist hits the campus, and if his critique of Rich is at all representative, apparently he stays home often. To know her politics is to know "where she's coming from" – which, for Epstein, is quite enough.

What matters more, however, is the way that liberals stack the deck in semiofficial volumes of literary history like the *Harvard*

Guide to Contemporary American Writing. By asking the question that also serves as the title of his essay – namely, "Is American Literature an Equal-Opportunity Employer?" – Epstein means to "have it out" with those who would divide the canon into neat but impossibly artificial categories: e.g., Black Writers, Women Writers, Jewish-American Writers, Homosexual Writers. Harvard should somehow *know* better, Epstein keeps implying, especially as one cliché-ridden essay follows on the heels of another.

But, Epstein also implies, half-baked thought is precisely what one might expect of the current crop of academic critics, and of a liberal bastion like Harvard. Indeed, we have become so accustomed to thinking about our writers in terms of race, sex, and ethnic identification that the very idea of a category called "Good Writing" would seem surprising, if not downright bizarre.

What, then, to do? Epstein tackles the problem by asking us to imagine Alberto D'Andrea, a young man studying American literature at the University of Rome. He has dutifully made his way through the Puritans and the great New England writers of the nineteenth century; he has studied Hawthorne and Melville, Twain and James, and has had a quick survey that touched on naturalism and early modernists like Fitzgerald, Hemingway, and Faulkner. Presumably he's ready to take on contemporary American writing, and he figures that the *Harvard Guide to Contemporary American Writing* will help.

Unfortunately, contemporary American literature seems to D'Andrea to be a confusing mishmash, hodgepodges piled atop hodgepodges:

> . . . There is black literature, of course, of which Alberto has heard, with black writers on the attack against American society, and then further divided among themselves. There is women's literature, speaking from, as the critics in the United States say, another consciousness, "another equally significant area of experience." There are realists, naturalists, novelists of manners, and experimental novelists by the score. There are Southern writers, deep fellows these, writing on the theme of self and history and something called "the awful re-

sponsibility of Time." Then there are the Jewish writers – Alberto pictures them in yarmulkes and prayer shawls – dreamy figures, trying to flee the responsibility of tradition, family, civilization, so that they can enjoy sex a bit more.

As Epstein's satiric persona, D'Andrea does a masterful job of giving the raspberry to dozens of well-regarded American critics. The snippets that D'Andrea (aka Epstein) selects are pretentious, trivial, often downright silly. Could the "experts" have gotten it all wrong?

Evidently so. For what emerges from the *Harvard Guide* is a portrait of American literature that steadfastly refuses to wrap itself in the flag, and to sing our national anthem with full throat:

> If all these writers, with all their special concerns and points of view, have one thing in common it is a grave unease in their own country. The *Harvard Guide*, Alberto cannot help but notice, claims over and over again that most American writers acutely feel a sense of powerlessness. In the words of one author discussed in the book, "America is a bitch." With his yellow-marker pen, Alberto D'Andrea draws a line under that sentence.

Here is a case – increasingly common among neoconservative essayists – in which history repeats itself with a difference, the difference being intellectual credentials, rhetorical skills, and ideological quarterlies like *Commentary*. To be sure, there have always been those who hankered for a more patriotic American literature, complete with positive portraits of kindly executives, satisfied citizens, and happy marriages, but the calls seldom bore the postmark of a department of English or the imprimatur of a *Commentary* magazine.

At stake, of course, is nothing less than the national imagination. By pulling down the vanities and the lavish [undeserved] praise that surround writers like Joyce Carol Oates, Thomas Pynchon, Robert Stone, John Irving, Ann Beattie et al., Epstein means to clear ground for, say, a James Gould Cozzens revival. No doubt there are contemporary writers for whom Epstein might work up a cheer or two, but I suspect that their politics would ultimately disappoint him.

Fascism, Hemingway once pointed out, is the politics of disappointed individuals; neoconservatives share something of this generalized sense of disappointment, without, of course, sharing in the totalitarian itch that make fascists so dangerous. In Epstein's case, he takes an almost giddy delight in counting the ways popular culture is turning sour. Take language, for instance. A gaffe in a student paper (what English professor does not have his or her favorite?) becomes yet another occasion to bash the liberals who are, it seems, responsible for every crime, including those perpetrated against the language:

> Poor Madame Bovary [Epstein begins], one understands and sympathizes with her condition. It is very awkward – if not so awkward as that of the freshman student at my university who, in a term paper, spotted the difficulty when he wrote: "Madame Bovary's problem is that she cannot make love in the concrete." How could he know that the word "concrete" is itself an abstraction, a by now quite stale metaphor, and one used in his unpracticed hand to hilarious effect? How could he know that for professors one of the few pleasures in grading student papers is that of writing zippy comments in the margins, and that he had set up his professor exquisitely? In his unconscious trope rendering Emma Bovary frigid in the concrete, the possibilities he provided for marginal comment – and comedy – were not practically but altogether boundless. Only the greatest restraint prevents me from trying out twenty or thirty such comments here myself.

But that much said by way of introduction, Epstein gets down to the more serious business at hand – namely, an investigation into why there is such a booming market for books like William Safire's *On Language* (1981) or John Simon's *Paradigms Lost* (1981). Part of the problem, of course, is that "language is under attack by feminists, by proponents of Black English and bilingualism, by homosexuals, and by a general resurgence of the populist strain in our culture." No doubt the general public, hungering for standards in an age that has knocked most of them into a cocked hat, figures that books on usage will perform the same social magic that Emily Post on etiquette did for earlier generations.

Unfortunately, the problem of language – like the other problems Epstein pinches his face about in *Plausible Prejudices* – comes down to politics, and more to the point, to liberal politics:

> . . . language itself has been under political attack for at least a decade now. Here feminists lead the way. Precision, elegance, good sense, all must fall before the feminist juggernaut, from doing away with any words suffixed with "man" to the creation of new pronouns. But it is not feminists alone who must be catered to linguistically. The *sine qua non* of contemporary speech and writing is that it give no possible offense. Books – and especially textbooks – are combed carefully for possible linguistic burrs. Among the minority groups whose sensibilities must be guarded is the group known as the college-attending ignorant. Thus a friend of mine, in preparing a textbook in art history, was told to eliminate the term "anti-bourgeois" – on the ground that it was too difficult for his intended undergraduate audience. One might as well be asked to write a cookbook without mentioning the word salt.

Epstein is, by any reckoning, a formidable writer. In an age where metaphysical jawbreakers dominate academic discourse and where the level of general speech is punctuated by "you know's," "OK's," and grunts, he can hold his own with a purist like John Simon (indeed, Epstein can even take him to task for the occasional verbal misfire in *Paradigms Lost*) without giving in to the sheer nastiness that often spoils Simon's prose.

In short, Epstein tries hard to come off as other than a linguistic snob. But his asides give him away. Here, for example, is Epstein on one of John Simon's pet projects: "an Academy of the Anglo-American Language." After concluding that this is an idea whose time is never likely to come in a democracy such as ours, Epstein explains why, and in ways that tell us more about bashing the Left than it does about linguistic niceties:

In a culture so intensely political as ours now is, creating such an Academy figures to be much more impossible than necessary. To cite but a single example, could such an Academy be formed without Noam Chomsky, the great name in linguistics in our day? Probably not. Yet I for one should not be pleased to see so politically engaged a man as Chomsky adjudicating questions of language; imagine him, for example, on the word "imperialism."

The reasonably good manners Epstein extends to Simon (a man who does not usually bring out this quality in others) screech to a halt when he imagines Chomsky as Language Czar. One wonders, though, if Epstein would be as quick to disqualify a Patrick Buchanan or a William F. Buckley – writers who know their way around a paragraph – on the ground that they, too, are "politically engaged"?

In fact, when Epstein takes our "politically intensive culture" to task, he often does so without realizing that his essays – and the magazines in which they appear – could be dragged into court as Exhibit A. No doubt Epstein would argue that the politics *he* means has an inordinate affection for the word "rights" – as in Gay Rights or Women's Rights or Whales' Rights. He would insist that there are no neoconservative bumper stickers, and that there is a mighty difference between the threadbare sloganeering of the Left and the erudition of a *Commentary* magazine.

| | |

Nonetheless, magazines like *Commentary* and the *New Criterion* suggest an atmosphere of sharply defined ideological positions. Every square inch of every issue – from its lead articles to its book reviews – contributes to the articulation of a neoconservative vision. In short, one does not open a new issue expecting surprises. This makes for a certain disadvantage among readers who are not True Believers, but it is a boon to those contributors who collect their essays between hard covers. Epstein was one beneficiary; Midge Decter is another. Beginning with *The Liberated Woman and*

Other Americans (1971) and continuing through collections like *The New Chastity and Other Arguments Against Women's Liberation* (1972) and *Liberal Parents, Radical Children* (1975), Dector has been a steady presence in the pages of *Commentary* – usually as one of feminism's chief detractors. That the magazine is edited by her husband, Norman Podhoretz, makes them look for all the world like an American equivalent of F. R. Leavis whose *Scrutiny* magazine often published articles by his wife, Queenie. In any event, what began as so much "prophecy" in *The Liberated Woman* – namely, that "It seems nowadays more acceptable to characterize oneself as the victim of a monstrosity, or even as a monster oneself, than as simply human. Apart from its terrifying arrogance, this attitude leaves us as a people gasping every five years for an understanding of what has happened since the last set of formulas captured our collective mind, and, in our breathlessness, empty and waiting for the next set to replace it" – gradually hardened, in the next collections, into neoconservative dogma. But this much said, let me hasten to add that Dector is hardly a Johanna One-Note. In recent years – again, in the pages of *Commentary* – Dector has made it clear that she is every bit the homophobe as others in the neoconservative camp ("The Boys on the Beach," *Commentary*, September 1980), and she has even taken her swipes at Irving Howe ("Socialism & Its Irresponsibilities: The Case of Irving Howe," *Commentary*, December 1982). Moreover, as the Executive Director of the Committee for a Free World and a trustee of the Heritage Foundation – neoconservative enterprises of the first water – she is a lady whose orbits ripple well beyond the editorial offices of *Commentary* magazine.

And yet, it is *Commentary* that published Dector's most controversial essays, and it is a safe bet that the Acknowledgments' page of her next book will reflect this simple but vitally important fact. What will *not* be acknowledged, however, are the subtle ways that Midge Dector and Norman Podhoretz have striven to assume the mantle, and the prominence, once worn so elegantly by Lionel and Diana Trilling. In many important ways, Lionel Trilling was the quintessential New York intellectual, and since his death in 1975 any number of cultural figures – on the Left as well as the Right –

have argued long and hard to anchor his ghost squarely in their camp. None, however, has been more energetic than Podhoretz.

From his student days at Columbia University, Podhoretz counted himself in Trilling's camp, although he will hasten to add that if Trilling were alive he would no doubt be making common cause with the neoconservatives. As Podhoretz's syllogism would have it: (a) neoconservatives are right-thinking folks (b) Trilling was no fool (ergo) Trilling would be a neoconservative. So much for Podhoretz's less-than-dazzling logic. Argue that it is easier to imagine a Trilling appalled by the steady drift toward the Right that *Commentary* has taken, that the cultural pronouncements Podhoretz makes with the certainty of a butcher cleaving meat were hardly Trilling's style, that being called a neo-*anything* would have offended his sensibility, and Podhoretz will point to the title of his 1986 book — appropriated from Trilling himself — and explain that

> Writers have been killed by politicians for expressing ideas of writing in certain ways; but (what is less often acknowledged) these same politicians have also been inspired by other writers to shed the blood of their fellow writers, and millions of nonwriters as well.

The nine essays collected in *The Bloody Crossroads* concentrate on the latter half of Podhoretz's syllogism about Trilling's equation, at that spot where writers meet, and sometimes embrace, the nightmare of communism. As Podhoretz argues, there may be two major forms of totalitarianism, but they are not equally insidious: ". . . Hitler inspired very few writers to apologize for his crimes against their fellow writers, let alone his crimes against any other groups or classes." Oh yes, there was Ezra Pound, there was Wyndam Lewis, there was Louis-Ferdinand Celine, but these writers strike Podhoretz as exceptions, as small potatoes. Because fascism is abhorrent to the liberal West, because it requires brute force for its successes, Podhoretz insists that even the Nazis at their worst were neither as insidious nor as dangerous as communism. Why so? Because communism has always depended on the "whole-hearted enthusiasm that countless writers have from the beginning felt and openly displayed" on its behalf.

In short, Podhoretz takes the gloves off early. He is an anti-Communist among anti-Communists, a man for whom four cheers is hardly sufficient to praise democratic capitalism. Thus it is no longer enough to denounce the Russian Revolution as *The God That Failed*, because as noteworthy, as spectacular, as that collection of essays by the likes of Arthur Koestler, Richard Wright, André Gide, and Ignazio Silone was, it did not tell the whole grisly tale. Why, Podhoretz asks, were writers like Max Eastman or Whittaker Chambers (*Whittaker Chambers?*) not included? Presumably because they would not fit into the chorus of testimony against communism from ex-Communists who had remained in some sense on the Left.

Podhoretz's point, one he drives toward over and over again, is that liberals have a nasty habit of replacing one dangerous illusion with another:

> . . . to reject Communism while trying to hold onto Marxism or socialism in some other form was – and is – intellectually insufficient. It left one in the position of blaming Stalin or Lenin or the special condition of Russia for the perversion or betrayal of the true heritage of Marxian socialism. In this way one remained free to go on believing in the utopian dreams of a transformed and redeemed world. Anyone under the sway of such utopian dreams was likely to evade the actual choices presented by reality in the here and now.

The result is a world neatly divided between those who cling to childish things and those with the courage to play hardball. Podhoretz sees the former under nearly every bed, the latter in the pages of journals like *Public Interest*, the *New Criterion*, and, of course, *Commentary*. The ostensible subject of a Podhoretz essay – whether it be the novels of Henry Adams or those of Milan Kundera – becomes less important than the consistent vision, the "editorial position," if you will, that he brings to them. No matter, for example, that a writer like Aleksandr Solzhenitsyn yearns for the return of a Czarist, and anti-Semitic, Russia; he is right-thinking about Israel (for Podhoretz, the acid – indeed, the *only* – test of anti-Semitism) and uncompromising about his anti-communism.

On the other hand, Henry Kissinger (whose books Podhoretz much admires: ". . . they have earned a place among the great books of their kind and among the great works of our time.") makes the fatal flaw of imagining the Soviet Union as simply another nation-state among nation-states, rather than as the "evil empire":

> Kissinger was so good at diplomacy, so great a virtuoso in the negotiating arts, that he may well have come to imagine that he could negotiate *anything*; and this may have led him into the mistake (which the intellectual in him could reinforce with dazzling rationalizations) of trying to negotiate the nonnegotiable.

As his "Revaluation" of F. R. Leavis suggests, Podhoretz developed his capacity for audacious judgments at the knee of a master. "The great English novelists," Leavis once pronounced, as if the mere uttering of the words made it so, "are Jane Austen, George Eliot, Henry James, and Joseph Conrad." By contrast, Podhoretz does his mentor one better by declaring that "If Orwell were alive today, he would be taking his stand with the neoconservatives and against the Left."

To be sure, Podhoretz has no monopoly on putting self-serving words into the mouth of the safely dead. Shakespeare – about whom we know precious little – has, at one time or another, been claimed by every religious group, every warmonger, every pacifist, every vegetarian, every certified crackpot on both sides of the Atlantic. This is not the case with Orwell. He conducted his education in public print, which is also to say that he frequently changed his mind. Cull the right quotes, and he becomes a liberal's darling; look at him from Podhoretz's perspective and he turns into a neoconservative.

As is so often with Podhoretz, this is a case of flinging a pebble into a pond and daring nine sages to find it. Orwell is, of course, in no position to argue Podhoretz's point, and this sage, for one, has no inclination to dive into such murky water. But it is worth pointing out that Orwell has, in effect, become Podhoretz's doppelgänger, the mirror-image of his own disaffection with the intellectual Left. Not only would Orwell be a neoconservative *today*, he was, in fact,

. . . a forerunner of neoconservatism in having been one of the first in a long line of originally left-wing intellectuals who have come to discover more saving and moral wisdom in the instincts and mores of "ordinary" people than in the ideas and attitudes of the intelligentsia.

There was a time when Podhoretz had a penchant for titles that relied heavily on the participle: *Doings and Undoings* (1964; contemporary literature reduced to a scorecard); *Making It* (1967; an account, partly confessional, partly celebratory, of how he clawed his way to the editorship of *Commentary*); *Breaking Ranks* (1979) (the why-and-how he became a neoconservative). In each case, the participle signaled process, a sense of ideas in flux. By contrast, *The Bloody Crossroads* makes it clear that the long arc of Podhoretz's career has brought him back, once again, to the 1950s, and to the Cold War that so divided the New York intellectuals. Small wonder that he has so much difficulty reading the novels of Milan Kundera (if they are not anti-Communist tracts, then what, he ponders, *are* they?) or that his revisionist portrait of Henry Adams takes him to task for his "alienation."

In short, one can nearly forgive Podhoretz his pontifications, his displeasure with the self-absorption of much contemporary fiction, and the mannered difficulty of much critical theory. But what is one to make of the Podhoretz who opposes federal funding for AIDS research on the ground that this will allow homosexuals to, in Podhoretz's mean-spirited, words, "bugger themselves with impunity." We have heard much about how Podhoretz differs from liberals, from democratic socialists, indeed from anyone to the left of center. Perhaps he will use the pages of *Commentary* to tell us in what ways he differs from, say, a Lyndon LaRouche. Those who miss the issue will, no doubt, be able to catch the essay the next time Podhoretz brings out a collection.

Modernist Culture, the Cunning of History, and Paul de Man

![decorative rule]

When relevations about Paul de Man's past first came to public attention last December, those on the attack as well as those for the defense found themselves turning to his influential *Allegories of Reading* (1979) in an effort to "read" de Man himself. Not surprisingly, what they found there was hardly conclusive:

> All that will be represented in such an allegory will deflect from the act of reading and block access to its understanding. The allegory of reading narrates the impossibility of reading. . . . Everything in this novel signifies something other than what it represents, be it consciousness, politics, or art.

Granted, de Man was talking about Proust's *Remembrance of Things Past* (1919), but he might as easily have been speaking to the contradictory, often elusive signifiers of his own life. For those writing in the popular press, the fact that de Man had contributed articles to collaborationist Belgian newspapers was disturbing enough; that his cultural pronouncements also included anti-Semitic echoes of the Nazi party line was devastating. But how to "read" this de Man in the context of the Yale professor many had come to know as an influential theoretician and teacher, how to conjoin signifiers with the signified remains a perplexing question. Allegories of indirection may well be the best way to proceed, given what we now know about de Man himself and what he has taught us about the "impossibility of reading."

| | |

New York City's West 47th Street is famous for its jewelry, its diamonds, and the cut-rate prices a savvy shopper can pick up on both. But the block between Broadway and Seventh Avenue – known as the Diamond Market – offers browsers more than large selections and discounted prices; those with a taste for the exotic will find glatt kosher food (available in everything from sit-down restaurants, three flights up, to rolling carts packed at the curbside) and, of course, the black-garbed Hassidic Jews who give the area its curious mixture of eighteenth-century Poland and fast-paced, competitive America.

To be sure, the Big Apple has blocks like this by the hundreds, places where disparate languages and ethnic lifestyles have learned – sometimes slowly, often reluctantly – to coexist. New Yorkers *kvetch* about cabbies who fracture the Mayor's English or about the high costs in time and money of special interest politics, but which of them would prefer the homogenized life readily available in, say, Sioux City, Iowa? Where would one go for sushi? for Thai? for a four-inch pastrami sandwich?

I belabor this point because New York City is a study in contradictions that have lived next to each for so long that the natives hardly notice. Take the block of West 47th Street I began with. True, that is where to go if you're in the market for a two-carat diamond or a cameo brooch. But it's also the block where one can find the Gotham Book Mart. For some sixty years, those looking for out-of-print modernist classics – a copy of, say, *Hommage à Proust* (1923) or back issues of *transition* – are likely to find them, squirreled away in one of its bulging shelves. The Gotham Book Mart's signboard proudly announces, *WISE MEN FISH HERE*, and, indeed, many do: authors, established and struggling; tenured professors and gypsy scholars; and, of course, students of all ages and condition.

What I want to explore in this essay, however, are not the curious juxtapositions that have become as much a part of city life as asphalt and grid lock, but, rather, the ways in which such conjunctions are becoming increasingly rare as the separation between quotidian life and intellectual design grows ever wider. I mean to talk, first, about general tendencies in modernist writers, and then to fix upon the career of Paul de Man as an example of history's terrible cunning and its high moral cost. I begin with a section from Robert Boyers's 1987 book, *After the Avant-Garde*:

> A number of influential critics argue that literary works do not represent the real world, that they are self-referential sign-systems with encoded meanings. Readers are said to work at these meanings with no sense that anything conclusive is at stake. Whatever may be thought to correspond to experience outside the given text will give itself away as an illusion to which trained readers will be fully resistant. How, after all, can a novel that organizes its material manage to represent what is at best random and intransigently elusive?

Once again, let our signs point back to West 47th Street, where some are spending the afternoon comparison shopping, others are thumbing through an out-of-print collection of T. S. Eliot's essays, and the ultra-Orthodox are whipping through their afternoon prayers. However, transport these images to the Antwerp of 1941 and you will have a very different story, one that has shocked and deeply divided American academics. I refer, of course, to the cause célèbre surrounding Paul de Man, the influential literary theoretician and, until his death in 1984, the Sterling Professor of Humanities at Yale University.

That literary critics have long jousted about which influences, which beliefs, which values, should matter most in establishing cultural hierarchies is hardly a revelation; nor are we surprised when it turns out that our most honored writers reflected what the community of scholars, critics, and reviewers – to say nothing of the society at large – felt was centrally important. When men of letters were comfortable, rather than embarrassed, about cultural standards, literature mattered because it *was* Life, albeit writ large and in bold, articulate relief. Modernism did much to overturn both the Victorian drawing room and the criticism that generated from its overstuffed armchairs. Virginia Woolf's famous claim that "On or about December 1910, human character changed" is simply one hyperbolic example among many. Whether it be abstract art or atonal music, theoretical physics or aesthetic theories, the NEW announced itself as series of shocks. No doubt Woolf had a specific set of cultural circumstances in mind – the death of Edward VII; London's Post-Impressionist exhibition – but what her playful remark really gets to is the impossibility of an Arnold Bennett rendering the interior life of a Mrs. Brown.

In short, literary modernism made strenuous efforts to disconnect itself from both the Romanticism and the Realism that were its immediate predecessors. Thus is it ever when Influence peers over the shoulder of the anxious, individual talent. But if literary modernists were dedicated to breaking windows so that fresh air might at last come in (one thinks of Whitman, of Lawrence, of Joyce), it is also true that theirs remained a quarrel about what Life was, and how it might be most authentically represented on the printed page. Granted, modernist works were difficult and demanding (indeed, that was one of their identifying characteristics); granted, they often valued stylistic considerations above all others; but, again, this was a response to the chaos, indeed, to the anarchy, of modern life itself. Myth – whether it came dressed in the allusions of Eliot's "waste land" or as Joyce's Homeric Dublin on June 16, 1904 – provided the necessary structures that allowed one to see modern life both steady and whole.

Thus far so good. Unfortunately, the revolutionary zeal of many literary modernists often stood foursquare against what Yeats called "the filthy democratic tide," and all too often took a dangerous tilt toward the political Right. "Common readers" became synonymous with the Great Unwashed, with all those who looked forward to what-comes-next, and to an omniscient author who was not timid about telling Dear Readers what it meant. What for some remained a snobbish elitism became for others a priestly, totalitarian mission.

In our country, Whitman sounded his barbaric yawp on behalf of a democratic populism so broadly based that one is hard pressed to imagine who might stand outside its mighty umbrella. He was, after all, the poet of women as well as men, of Blacks as well as Whites, of the Jew as well as the gentile, of farmers as well as city folk, of the downtrodden as well as the rich. His European counterparts felt differently; for them, foreign elements corrupted rather than enriched.

Granted, not all American writers were as egalitarian or as welcoming as Whitman. In the horse race of American literature, one's place of birth, one's breeding, one's alma mater, always counted for a good deal – as the 1,200+ pages of the recent *Columbia Literary History of the United States* reminds us. There were those, then and now, who tried mightily to write off immigrant populations in a single, excoriating word: *threat*. Others were more thoughtful about their discomforts, feeling that while the "old orders" which had formed them were, indeed, under siege, the sheer potential of these "huddled masses" was inextricably linked to the larger democratic dream they continued to cherish.

For example, during his 1904 visit to America, the magisterial Henry James found himself overwhelmed by the physical reality of so many Yiddish-speaking immigrants squeezed into New York's tiny East Side, and Henry Adams – who felt his grip on the levers of American power slipping even more than James did – made these comments about the Washington, D.C., of 1914:

> The atmosphere really has become a Jew atmosphere. It is curious and evidently good for some people, but it isolates me. I do not know the language, and my friends are as ignorant as I. We are still in power, after a fashion. Our sway over what we call society is undisputed. We keep Jews far away, and the anti-Jew feeling is quite rabid. We are anti-everything and we are wild up-lifters; yet we somehow seem to be more Jewish every day.

My point, however, is not to call the roll of those American writers who were infected by garden varieties of anti-Semitism, nor is it to argue that every writer from Socrates to Styron be judged by a litmus test administered by the ADL. Rather, I want to concentrate on the implications of literary vision, and especially on the ways in which metaphor contributes to this power.

I begin with what once passed for universal wisdom – namely, that in learning to read our best literature, one learned to read oneself. To be sure, one pays attention to a writer's particulars – to Faulkner's South or Bellow's Chicago – and to the human beings one finds there, but the orbits of a literary work always ripple outward, to larger significances, and to the world readers meet when they turn the last page. To claim, as many now do, that literature refers to nothing outside itself, that it is both self-contained and self-referential, is to substitute a set of abstractions for a reader's experience, for literature's enormous power, and for the responsibility that is inextricably attached to both. In this sense, metaphor shares at least some properties with the life it draws its sustenance from and points to – and of these, perhaps the most important is moral consequence. When, for example, Sylvia Plath argues that Daddy is a Nazi and she a Jew, when she imagines German as a language that chuffs her off "like a Jew./A Jew to Dachau, Auschwitz, Belsen," the effect may be to magnify her psychological pain, to render an Electra complex in the strongest, starkest terms possible, but the hyperbole comes at a certain cost – namely, the trivialization of history. The effect, in a word, is obscene, and ultimately numbing.

Plath's "Daddy" is, to be sure, an instance of history appropriated to the purely personal, and in that sense it speaks to latter-day Romanticism as one of our heartier perennials. But in our century the more typical situation has been directed toward erasing the "un" in Shelley's nineteenth-century claim that "Poets are the unacknowledged legislators of the world." Nearly forty years ago America's intellectual community deeply divided over the decision to award Ezra Pound a Bollingen Prize for his *Pisan Cantos*. To his enduring credit, Karl Shapiro voiced his "No! in thunder" as a Bollingen judge (the only one, by the way, to do so), and others – Clement Greenberg, William Barrett, Irving Howe – argued vigorously that Pound's anti-Semitism was so incrusted in the fabric of his poetry, so much a part of his aesthetic, that the two were inseparable. Others, schooled in, and committed to, the autonomy of Art, felt that a writer's politics had no place in a discussion of poetic excellence. The result had the look, even the feel, of an academic debate, albeit one held between clenched teeth. But there was nothing particularly academic about lines like the following:

the Yidd is a stimulant, and the goyim are cattle
in gt/proportion and go to saleable slaughter
with the maximum of docility.

To scan such lines with loving attention to the lilts and nuances of language, to comment about thematic patterns and image clusters is to talk about everything but the painfully obvious and humanly important. Still reeling from the blows dealt to their fellow Jews in the Holocaust, indeed, still reeling from the nightmare of fascism, how could responsible intellectuals keep silence?

| | |

The Pound case is, as they say, so much history, but history has a way of repeating itself – always, to be sure, with a difference, and never in the same neatly focused ways. As Marx knew full well, the tragedies of history have a nasty habit of repeating themselves as farce. Recently, more than a hundred pieces of journalism (book reviews, drama and music criticism, cultural speculations, and the like) written in Belgian newspapers during 1941–42 have been discovered and translated into English. That the pieces – like the Flemish and French newspapers in which they first appeared – reflect a general viewpoint that can only be called collaborationist is hardly surprising; that a handful of them reflect the blatantly anti-Semitic perspective that has often been a prominent feature of literary modernism is equally predictable. What *is* shocking, however, is that these mini-essays should turn out to have been written by Paul de Man, one of the principal architects of deconstruction and a man widely revered for his urbanity, his grace, his wide learning, and, above all else, for his views about the indeterminacy of language. As Gerald L. Bruns wrote recently:

[Paul de Man] argues that language is not a logical system for constructing descriptions of an independent reality but a historicized totality of texts – call them philosophy, science, literature, law, religion, literary criticism – within which what gets counted as reality is in a state of constant, interminable, aporetic redescription.

Deconstruction took the world of academic symposia, specialist journals, and rarefied coffee klatches by storm. Indeed, the English Department of Yale University – widely regarded as the Hot Center not only for deconstruction, but also for all things theoretical, densely written, and made originally in France – gained a national visibility that made outsiders jealous and insiders skittish. Those who always had their doubts about the wide net that indeterminacy presumably casts, or who regarded the erudite talk about "texts" as so much philosophical babble, seized upon the de Man relevations as an excuse to bash away at this latest assault on humanistic learning. Deconstruction struck R. W. B. Lewis, professor of American Studies at Yale, as antihistorical: "It encourages skepticism about almost anything in the realm of human experience. That's one of the things I hold against it." Others took the occasion to kick critical theorists while they were down. One anonymous wag, referring to the deconstructionist habit of treating all events – including war – as "texts," quipped: "Tell that to the Veterans of Foreign Texts." Unfair, perhaps, but wickedly near the mark, for deconstructionists wrench the universe itself into the realm of the unknown.

In short, no verbal construct – be it a poem or a political manifesto, an ad for Lite beer or Augustine's *Confessions* – could be trusted. Deconstructionists learned, above all, to raise tough philosophical questions, to turn all manner of assumptions either inside out or onto their heads. They, above anyone else, should not find it surprising that many feel there is a measure of poetic justice in the questions now being raised about one of the movement's major voices.

But that said, the attempts to link what a twenty-two-year-old Paul de Man wrote during the Belgium occupation and what he wrote as a Yale professor are exercises either in futility (for those seeking hard evidence of residual anti-Semitism) or in ingenuity (for those not adverse to turning de Man's deconstructionist method against his ghost). To my mind, it is more disturbing that many of de Man's colleagues – including some who now feign "shock" about his collaborationist past – were aware, at least in outline, of the articles recently unearthed. Indeed, this is a case where the all too familiar formula of "what did you know, and when did you learn it?" may yet find its way into the groves of academe. One thing, at least, is clear: the era of the cover-up is over, and those, however well-meaning their intentions, who urged de Man *not* to go public about his past will have much to answer for.

Which brings me to the cunning of history, a more venerable phenomenon than indeterminacy, and one with at least as many faces. Consider, for example, the following passage from de Man's March 4, 1941, article entitled *"Les Juifs dans la Littérature actuelle"* ("Jews in Contemporary Literature"):

> It shows the strength of our Western intellectuals [de Man argues] that they could protect, from Jewish influence, a sphere as representative of the culture at large as literature. . . [Thus] despite the lingering Semiticism in all our civilization, literature showed that its essential nature was healthy. . . [Nonetheless], a solution to the Jewish problem that aimed at the creation of a Jewish colony isolated from Europe would entail no deplorable consequences for the literary life of the Occident.

Granted, this is the most offensive, the most shivery square inch of prose in all of de Man's wartime journalism; and, not surprisingly, these are the lines that the popular press fastened upon. Precisely eighteen months later (on August 4, 1942), the first trainload of Belgian Jews left the country, headed for Auschwitz. Read with hindsight — and surely that must have a place in the reader-response arsenal — who would wish to argue that de Man's judgments made nothing happen, that they were as isolated and as purely literary as Auden's description of poetry itself: "it survives/In the valley of its making where executives/Would never want to tamper"? In wartime Europe, busy German executives did, indeed, want to tamper — and the plans they hatched for a Final Solution depended in equal measures on bureaucratic efficiency, on technological capability, and, not least of all, on the world's cooperation. Some had eyes but did not see the handwriting on the wall, the yellow stars sewn onto Jewish coats; some had ears but did not hear the sounds of shattered glass on *Kristallnacht*; and some, like de Man, poured old poisons into new bottles.

In this regard, the Belgian Paul de Man was hardly the dazzling, original thinker who became such a major force in contemporary literary theory. Rather, he represented the cultural mainstream of that time, that place. As Ortwin de Graef, the young Belgian scholar whose dissertation precipitated the de Man controversy, told me:

> It was, of course, a long established fact that the Jewish diamond industry exerted great economic power. And there is a way in which the fact that Marx was a Jew was a threat to a country like Belgium that was still Catholic. Indeed, there was a way in which Jews and Bolsheviks and capitalists were all linked together, and not very much liked at the time. In short, you had the Jewish-Bolshevik-capitalist conspiracy, however incongruous the notion might seem. But there is a way in which a scapegoat had to be found, and the Jews were an eligible target.

> Moreover, there's never smoke without fire. There is a way in which the Jews *did* play a certain role in economic manipulations that led to various international conflicts at the time.

De Graef is, of course, yet another instance of the ways in which the cunning of history has fastened itself to the ongoing saga of Professor de Man. The alternating currents of attack and defense that have swirled around de Man's legacy were the last things de Graef imagined possible when he began his scholarly research into the archives of Antwerp's Flemish community. An Antwerp native himself, de Graef knew that Hendrik de Man (Paul's uncle) was a prominent socialist, the author of an important critique of Marxism, *Zur Psychologie des Socialismus* (1926), and a member of the Zeeland government during the Nazi occupation. Perhaps he might find a reference to Paul de Man in the documentation about his more famous uncle.

What he found, instead, was a catalog listing for P. de Man, and the rest is controversy piled atop controversy. Had de Graef consciously set out to tarnish de Man's reputation, he could not have found more damaging evidence; but the irony – the cunning of history, if you will – is that he set about to light one more candle on de Man's altar. Again, in de Graef's own words:

> The issue of anti-Semiticism is very complicated in Belgium. De Man was from Antwerp, after all, and Antwerp is where the Jews of Belgium are largely concentrated. Moreover, they are a very particular type of Jew – isolated and "queer" for the native Belgian. . . . There was certainly an exclusivism, a racism, on the part of Belgian Jewry. Nor is it improbable that the Belgian Jews – certainly the Antwerp Jews – would, indeed, pray to Jehovah to "confound the *goyim*," as the illustration put it in *Le Soir*. So, when de Man talks about creating a separate colony for Jews outside of Europe, this is the very same idea that Jews themselves had been propagating for a long time – namely, the Zionist ideal of a Jewish colony in a Jewish country. What de Man said was this: *we're* European, and Jews, insofar as they profess themselves to be Jews, are not European.

In short, the diamond market of Antwerp – then and now – is regarded very differently from its counterpart on 47th Street. On the other side of the Atlantic, opinions that we would dismiss as fulminations from the lunatic fringe retain a disturbing currency.

Many factors account for the difference, but certainly the democratic vision I spoke about earlier is the most important. Indeed, here one sees the cunning of history in its most complicated, and most tragic, form. For what broke down in the prewar Belgium of its best intellectuals was a belief in liberal democracy. In the salon life of Brussels (where the young Paul de Man was an active participant), nothing was more certain than the bankruptcy of liberalism in general, and the present Belgian order in particular. No doubt de Man's Flemish – as opposed to Walloon – roots intensified his reactionism.

By 1939, Hendrik de Man believed that only an "authoritarian" democracy could bring about Socialist reform; a year later, the Nazis invaded Belgium, and he entered into his ill-fated "collaboration of principle" with the occupier. As Jean Stengers, editor of *Revue Belge de Philologie et d'Histoire*, recounts the series of tragic decisions and their consequences:

[In 1939, Hendrik de Man] wanted governments set up for four years, during which time parliament would not be permitted to overthrow them; budgets voted for four years; and one chamber instead of the bicameral system. At the same time, he renewed his earlier proposals for a corporatist system that would have its say in economic questions. World War II came before these views could be discussed by the Socialist Party itself. In the country they found very little echo. But after the German victory of May and June, 1940, de Man's loss of faith in democracy had a direct result. As president of the Socialist Party, he then issued a manifesto celebrating the collapse of "decrepit" democracies as a "liberation" for the working class. A short spell of collaboration with the Germans ensued; but de Man did not find much more comfort there. He ended his life an exile in Switzerland. He had no disciples.

To be sure, Hendrik de Man was hardly alone either in his despair about the Nazi juggernaut or in his hope that Socialists might be able to "bore from within" their ranks; as fantastic as it now seems, the condition affected a great many European intellectuals who felt defeated by history and who hoped that fascism might provide a route toward cultural renewal. Thus, Hendrik de Man argued that while Hitler is some sort of demonic, violent force, and while he couldn't be at all sure about the Europe that might emerge, a Hitler *might* be necessary.

In Hendrik de Man's case, New Ideas did not goose-step into the country wearing a Nazi uniform. There was never a blind embracing of Sturm und Drang, no enthusiasm for the pan-Aryan ideal, no passion for the swastika. But there was a strong feeling that the new order offered a way out of the dead end of Belgian politics, and that one could imagine an independent Belgium, and a stronger Europe, when the process completed itself. In this case, the "one" – be it Hendrik de Man or his nephew, Paul – could not have been more tragically wrong.

Indeed, what we have as the de Man affair forces us to concentrate on wartime Belgium as a series of threadbare semantic distinctions: collaborationists of principle vs. simple collaborationists; cultural anti-Semitism with a modernist patina vs. an anti-Semitism fully prepared to act on its convictions. That Paul de Man's last years were spent teaching us to distrust language, to see the inexorable ways in which politics fastens itself around claims of value in literature or in the very rhythms of what we call history is perhaps the final irony that history itself has in mind for his epitaph.

Lost Causes /
Marginal Hopes:
The Collected Elegies of
Irving Howe

God died in the nineteenth century,
utopia in the twentieth.
from Irving Howe's *A Margin*
of Hope

At one point in *A Margin of Hope* (1982), Irving Howe's intellectual autobiography, he speaks of himself as "moving closer to the secular Yiddish milieu at the very moment it was completing its decline" – and then he wonders, almost as an afterthought, if this newfound passion is not perhaps "another lost cause added to my collection." Such candor on Howe's part has hardly been in short supply; indeed, it is precisely this ability to look upon both the world and the self with a critical, often skeptical, detachment – and to report the results with an unflinching honesty – that have been the hallmarks of his eloquent, forceful style. In the long arc of his career – as political radical, as polemicist, as editor, as educator, as literary critic, and, not least of all, as *writer* – there have, indeed, been lost causes aplenty, and, perhaps more important, countless opportunities to mourn their passing, to reflect on their respective failures, to sit *shiva* in elegantly formed paragraphs.

For Howe – and, one might add, for much of American literature – nothing quite succeeds like failure, or failing that, the intellectually bracing aroma of fallen grandeur. As a very young, young man, Howe had known the giddy excitement of editing – and, in truth, doing much of the writing – for *Labor Action*, a Socialist publication longer on certainty and argumentation than it was on irony. As Howe remembers it, he

> . . . lived by the excitement of turning out this four-page weekly. . . . It was the best training of my life and one of the happiest periods, too. . . . Prolific and cocksure, brimming with energy and persuaded I had a key to understanding the world, I needed only the reams of yellow paper on which I typed and the *New York Times* from which to draw facts. (Blessed *New York Times*! What would radical journalism in America do without it?)

He was all of twenty-one years old at the time, but circumstance, inclination, considerable talent, and, yes, let us admit it, luck had turned him into a Socialist to be reckoned with. By his own admission, Howe had become a Socialist "at the advanced age of fourteen"; the East Bronx had been his teacher, but Howe would be the first to insist that his was hardly an extraordinary education: those with eyes to see and hearts to feel came to similar conclusions about the way the world was, and might become.

City College deepened his convictions, sharpened his political skills – not in its classrooms (which more often than not, Howe found boring or irrelevant, if he showed up at all) – but, rather, in the now-famous debates that pitted the Socialists of Alcove 1 against the Communists of Alcove 2. The Communists, as Sherwood Anderson once pointed out, "*meant* it," and while Howe was sharp enough to see how large a role ideological fixities played in their passionate certainty, he was also vulnerable enough to see that his penchant for abstract thought, for elaborately nuanced argument, came with liabilities as well as assets.

The more interesting question, then – and one Howe poses to himself in *A Margin of Hope* – is why a Socialist, rather than a Communist? After all, in 1934 the Communists were more numerous, more active, more fashionable. They, rather than the Socialists, sat smugly in history's catbird seat. Perhaps it was, as Howe suggests, simply a matter of timing: the Socialists got to him first.

Or perhaps it was that "Jewish Socialism" – a phenomenon Howe describes as "not merely politics or an idea, [but rather] an encompassing culture" – contained more of the life actually lived among immigrant Jews – more of its rhythms, its ironic quips and deep-seated skepticisms, its *Weltschmerz* and compassion.

But one also suspects that long before Howe encountered *Moby-Dick* he was destined to number himself among the world's "loose-fish." There are those who bristle at the discipline that politics often demands and those who find it oddly comforting. Howe discovered early that his divided temperament embraced both positions. Still, "the trouble with politics," Oscar Wilde once quipped, "is that it takes up one's evenings." One could argue that politics consumed a goodly portion of Howe's energy, and his life. And if the bald truth be told, only in those moments – short-lived and nostalgically recalled – when he threw himself heart-and-soul into the "movement" did the sheer tedium, the petty bickering, seem worthwhile:

> Never, before, and surely never since, have I lived at so intense a pitch, or been so absorbed in idea beyond the smallness of self. It began to seem as if the very shape of reality could be molded by our will, as if those really attuned to the inner rhythms of History might bend it to submission.

Granted, even this giddy time of boundless confidence and selfless commitment did not come without costs – a certain narrowness of focus, a honing of skills longer on argumentation than on substance, a penchant for moral smugness. In such a world – with its internecine squabbles and unshakeable convictions – what one did, above all else, was "take positions." For Howe, nothing seemed more evident during the Depression than the simple, everywhere observable fact that history itself had reached a point of crisis, that capitalism was in its death throes.

Years later, of course, Howe would admit that capitalism turned out to be more resilient than he had reckoned (his was "by no means a fatuous conclusion in the thirties, only a mistaken one"), but that is only to say he had not figured either on Franklin Delano

Roosevelt's shrewd ability to deflect revolutionary ardor with modest economic reforms, or on the willingness of so many workers – including trade unionists – to accept them.

Granted, one savored those moments when history confirmed the prophetic wisdom of this-or-that radical position – the Trotskyites were "right" about the Moscow trials, "right" about the Soviet Union, "right," in a word, about Stalin – but all too often their arguments were no match when pitted against simpler, thrillingly melodramatic scenarios. The Spanish Civil War provided an instructive case in point. As Howe points out in *A Margin of Hope*:

> The most cogent of the issues raised by the anti-Stalinist Left had to do with democratic rights within Loyalist Spain, the way the NKVD, the Russian secret police, had taken over an increasing share of police powers. We were saying what George Orwell would say in *Homage to Catalonia* – a book that earned him a hail of scorn. Our criticism had a moral rationale but was politically very difficult, perhaps impossible, at a time when fascism had taken over most of Europe and the socialist spirit was in full retreat. We were complicating the Spanish question in ways that seemed insufferable. That the loyalist Spain which so stirred hearts could also be guilty of allowing the NKVD to kidnap and murder Andres Nin, the POUM leader, was simply too much. People could not bear to hear that La Passionaria, the flaming defender of Madrid, was also a ruthless Stalinist persecuting political opponents. People could not bear to hear that even in loyalist Spain there was reason to dismay, cause for grief.

Nonetheless, it was socialism's peculiar destiny – its fate, if you will – to be the bearer of complicated, and complicating, news. Howe's own position in the movement, especially as its numbers and influence dwindled into what might more accurately be described as a sect, was doubly complicated because he was an intellectual in a country that tolerates, even sometimes encourages, dissent, but that does not take it seriously: "We were driven back [Howe explains in retrospect] to a position somewhat resembling that of the nineteenth-century utopian Socialists: isolated critics without a social base." Such isolation is, of course, intolerable for those committed to radical politics; but it can be a boon, perhaps even a necessity, to the reading and sustained reflection that produces literary essays. In Howe's case, the line between literature and politics, between what he calls "intellectual salvage operations" and versions of autobiography was never sharply defined; the passions of the streets expressed themselves at the writing desk. To be sure, these opposite tugs – nearly always studies in contradiction – fused brilliantly in *Politics and the Novel* (1957), but, even here, Howe would insist on the necessary autonomy of the literary imagination, on establishing a clear line of difference between those who felt that literature is the servant of ideology (e.g., the vulgar Marxist criticism practiced by those who wrote for the Communist *New Masses*) and his own view that a "political novel" comes into view when the novelist's attention begins "to shift from the gradations within society to the fate of society itself."

And yet, for all Howe's combativeness and political savvy, one has the sense that there is an important part of him that prefers the beauty, and the quiet, of aesthetic contemplation. His collaborations with Eliezer Greenberg, for example – which produced such important anthologies of Yiddish literature as *Voices from the Yiddish* (1972) and the "treasuries" of Yiddish poetry and stories – began as yet another "salvage" job, an attempt to preserve a once-vibrant culture at its point of extinction, but to hear Greenberg actually *read* the poems of Mani Leib and Moshe Leib Halpern, of Jacob Glatstein, and then to argue about this nuance, that twist of translation, was a respite that required no lofty rationalization. Remembering those afternoons (which began in 1953 and stretched through the turbulent 1960s) Howe put it this way:

There was a pleasure in doing something absolutely pure – arguing over a recalcitrant idiom, measuring the suitability of a story for linguistic transformation, trying to cajole an underpaid translator to give "a little more blood." Our working together in the late sixties became for me a source of happiness

– one day a week away from the Vietnam war and the polemics with leftist ideologues into which I had locked myself.

| | |

If it is true that Howe, like other New York intellectuals, made a specialty of *not* being a specialist, if his career is a study of energy spread over a wide variety of interests and disciplines, it is also true that his is a life in which the word "accident" must be used with caution, and with quotation marks. I mentioned earlier that Howe began collaborating with Greenberg in 1953. Howe tells a part of the story in *A Margin of Hope*: he had reviewed a collection of Sholom Aleichem's stories in *Partisan Review*, and Greenberg had sent him a note, saying, first, that he liked the piece and, second, that they should "become partners." Normally, one keeps such "offers" at a healthy arm's length, but this one struck psychic paydirt. Howe went to see him, unsure as to what this partnership might consist of, and the rest is history.

But there was a prehistory as well – and for that one must imagine an Irving Howe just beginning to establish himself with the New York crowd and anxious to review books for, say, *Partisan Review*. Enter Philip Rahv, the legendary gruff-neck who ran *Partisan Review* with an iron fist and an icy wit. Or more correctly, enter the Irving Howe who was ushered into the journal's office and then asked to scan a shelf of review copies in the event that a book might strike his fancy. Here is a case where possibilities really are dizzying, where the moment's choice might spell the difference between success and failure. Howe chose Sholom Aleichem, Rahv smiled his approval, and the wheels that would grind slowly toward *World of Our Fathers* were set into motion.

Accident? Hardly. Indeed, one could argue that the story really started much, much earlier – in Howe's painful, ambivalent memories of his Yiddish-speaking childhood, and in the extraordinary piece he wrote about it called "The Lost Young Intellectual." In seeking to describe "a new social type" – the author who has published a few stories, perhaps even a novel, and who reviews books for obscure magazines; the painter whose pictures do not reach public view; the leader of a revolutionary political group with few followers; and, most of all, "the unattached intellectual who can function neither as creator nor politician because he is either frustrated and barren in his cultural pursuits or disillusioned with politics" – Howe was, at one and the same time, giving expression to a general condition and a portrait of himself.

As the essay's subtitle would have it, a man such as this is both "marginal" and "twice alienated":

> Usually born into an immigrant Jewish family, he teeters between an origin he can no longer accept and a desired status he cannot attain. He has largely lost his sense of Jewishness, of belonging to a people with a meaningful tradition, and he has not succeeded in finding a place for himself in the American scene or the American tradition.

To be sure, Howe invented neither the condition nor the term "alienation" – and, to his credit, he did not crusade on its behalf. Earlier, Delmore Schwartz's "In Dreams Begin Responsibilities" (*Partisan Review*, 1937), Isaac Rosenfeld's *Passage from Home* (1946), and Saul Bellow's *Dangling Man* (1944) had explored much the same Zeitgeist, and later the task of making the word itself fashionable, then widely popular, then finally devalued, fell to others in the *Partisan Review* crowd.

But it was Howe who best understood how this peculiar brand of alienation operated on the heart's field, how its "ambiguous compound of rejection and nostalgia" led to blockage and grief, but also to the possibility of an elegiac mode that could encompass both the pangs of history and the pain of self. In this regard, a vignette from "The Lost Young Intellectual" – and one Howe repeats in *World of Our Fathers* – is especially revealing:

> When I was a few years older, about eight or nine, my parents had a grocery store in an "Americanized" Jewish neighborhood, the West Bronx. I used to play in an abandoned lot about a block away from the store, and when I'd neglect to come home at supper time, my father would come to call for me. He would shout my name from afar, giving it a Yiddish

twist: "Oivee!" I would always feel a sense of shame at hearing my name so mutilated in the presence of amused onlookers, and though I would come home – supper was supper! – I would always run ahead of my father as if to emphasize the existence of a certain distance between us. In later years I often wondered how I would react if my father were again to call "Oivee" at the top of his lungs in, say, Washington Square.

One cites these painful lines without being quite sure how to describe this mixture of bravado and self-laceration, this subtle blending of irony and indignation, this laying bare of the conflicts that raged – admittedly, on less discerning, less articulate levels – between American sons and immigrant fathers. Never shy about turning his analytical skills inward, Howe wrote himself down as "*a victim of his own complexity of vision*: even the most harrowing of his feelings, the most intolerable aspects of his alienation, he must still examine with the same mordant irony he applies to everything else." Although it might, in Hemingway's famous words, "be pretty to think so," nice Jewish-boys are not likely to rebel by floating down the East River on a raft. Supper *is* supper, and postures (including alienation) are postures. So one does what one can – in this case, Howe writes "The Lost Young Intellectual." But one must also learn to live on in the full knowledge of one's age and its defining burdens. In this manner, Howe's composite intellectual "can find consolation and dignity, however, in the consciousness of his vision, in the awareness of his complexity, and the rejection of self-pity. To each age its own burdens."

"The Lost Young Intellectual" has the ring of manifesto about it, albeit one less fueled by revolutionary zeal than by a sense of impasse and cultural despair. But for all its handwringing – one suspects, for example, that Howe was always far more rooted in Jewishness than he lets on – this early essay introduced the themes, or in Howe's case, the causes for lament, that he would explore more fully later.

Consider, for example, the strains as well as the estrangement that Yiddish caused for those who spoke *mamaloshen* in their parent's kitchen and King's English in the public kindergarten. As

Howe relates one particularly chilling moment, it is easy, perhaps *too* easy, for us to imagine the humiliated five-year-old consigning Yiddish forever to the ashcan of History:

> Like many other Jewish children, I had been brought up in a constricted family environment, especially since I was an only child, and at the age of five really knew Yiddish better than English. I attended my first day of kindergarten as if it were a visit to a new country. The teacher asked the children to identify various common objects. When my turn came she held up a fork and without hesitation I called it by its Yiddish name "a *goopel.*" The whole class burst out laughing at me with that special cruelty of children. That afternoon I told my parents that I had made up my mind never to speak Yiddish to them again. . . .

Rather like Howe's "confession" about racing home past his immigrant father, his vow to forsake Yiddish was forged more in ambivalence than in theatre; the truth is that the longest journeys often end where they began. The same paradox often applies to the denials that turn into affirmations.

To be sure, *World of Our Fathers* is not "affirmation" as most rabbis understand, and use, the term. It is an encyclopedic, meticulously researched account of the immigrant Jewish world; it is a tale with epic grandeur and tragic sweep; it is, indeed, an intellectual "salvage job" of the first water. But it is also autobiography. By telling the story of the world that European Jews fled, and the world they found, and made, in America, Howe comes to better understand himself.

Does this mean that he "solved" the nagging problem of his Jewishness? Of course not, although that is precisely the yardstick commonsensical, pragmatic Americans prefer. Howe knows better. One hopes to *find* a problem, and by exploring it for its own sake, to discover things infinitely more precious than "programs":

> My own hope [Howe explains] was to achieve some equilibrium with that earlier self which had started with childhood Yiddish, my language of naming, and then turned away in

adolescent shame. Yiddish poetry, somber or wild, brought me no comprehensive views about "the Jewish problem," but it did something more valuable. It helped me to strike a truce with, and then extend a hand to, the world of my father.

But that much said about Howe and secular Yiddish, let me hasten to add that this alienated young man also suffered loneliness and isolation on the political front. As Howe put it in what would virtually become the New York intellectuals' anthem: "With the appearance of the depression, and the decline of large sections of the intelligentsia to marginal and often lumpen status, our intellectual could no longer feel security or strike roots; he has today become the most atomized member of an increasingly atomized society." To be sure, much of this generalized disenfranchisement would dissipate during the 1950s, but for Howe certain questions continued to nag: Why had American socialism failed? What had literary modernism meant? And later, Could one be a "loose-fish" *and* a tenured professor?

| | |

Let me suggest, first, that these questions are more intimately related than they appear to be at first glance. To write critical studies of Sherwood Anderson or William Faulkner, books out to prove that the son of an immigrant could take on heavyweight American authors, was, on one level, an act of chutzpah. For Howe, critical reading required little more than a focused concentration and a pencil. Others, however, were less sanguine. And what the raised eyebrows and whispers finally came down to was this: Could the son of an immigrant be trusted to teach, and to write about, American literature?

In the case of the book on Faulkner, other factors muddied the branch waters. There were whole worlds of difference — in politics, in demeanor, in style — between the New Critics who clustered around Nashville and the New York intellectuals. Granted, those most associated with *Partisan Review* also published their criticism in *Kenyon Review*, and as Howe told me recently their quarrels about literature had the advantage of being conducted "in English" – which is to say, both groups reacted to books, rather than "texts," and talked about them in understandable language, rather than in a heavy-water jargon.

Still, there must have been a sense that some people had squatter's rights to Faulkner while others had to learn about grits in the library stacks. Howe, of course, belonged squarely in the latter camp. He grew up with people who drank celery tonic, not Dr. Pepper; there were other "Irvings" in his neighborhood, but not, I suspect, a single Joe Bob. In short, there must have been some hangers-on in Nashville who regarded Howe as a literary carpetbagger.

Granted, none of this should matter, and for the best of the New York intellectuals and for the most impressive of the New Critics, it did not. Both groups agreed wholeheartedly with T. S. Eliot's position that all a critic really needs is "intelligence." Howe might miss a Southern nuance here, a whiff of verbena there, but even his most grudging critic would admit that he was a perceptive reader and a persuasive writer. After all, if the central question for apologist Southern writers was "How could God allow us to lose the War?" and the agony that modernist Southern writers struggled with was "Why do you hate the South?" Howe had been pondering similar questions – albeit, in another country – all his life.

Not surprisingly, then, the Faulkner that most interested Howe was the one who shared his passion for elegy, for missions of retrieval and rescue. For what are novels like *The Sound and the Fury* and *Absalom, Absalom!* if not exercises in lamentation, written at the moment when cultural residue and cultural extinction occupied the same uneasy space? And, for that matter, what is Eliot's *The Waste Land*, modernism's quintessential epic, but an extended lament for the redemptive rhythms that afflict industrial societies in the ambivalent space between "memory and desire"?

My point is simply that the energies that Howe plowed into the making of *World of Our Fathers* were not unlike the energies he expended on behalf of Faulkner or what he called "The Idea of the Modern." But here again, Howe found himself attracted – or perhaps more correctly, chosen – by subjects he came to "late," when traditions were breaking apart rather than in formation. As he put it in "The New York Intellectuals" – an account of writers such as Meyer Schapiro, Harold Rosenberg, Sidney Hook, and Lionel Abel, and of those times, that place they shared – their essays flowed less from a definable tradition than from a nagging sense of its passing:

> The great battles for Joyce, Proust, and Eliot had been fought in the twenties and mostly won; now, while clashes with entrenched philistinism might still occur, these were mostly mopping-up operations. The New York intellectuals came toward the end of the modernist experience, just as they came at what may yet have to be judged the end of the radical experience, and as they certainly came at the end of the immigrant Jewish experience. One quick way of describing their situation, a cause of both their feverish brilliance and recurrent instability, is to say that *they came late.*

Indeed, one could argue that the New York intellectuals missed out on virtually everything *but* the essay; and more, that their appetite for polemical argument, for dazzling analyses, for verbal pyrotechnics, helped to redefine what the literary essay was, and could be.

Perhaps nothing says more about the current literary scene than the spate of book-length studies about the New York intellectuals. There is, for example, Alexander Bloom's *Prodigal Sons* (1986), Terry A. Cooney's *The Rise of the New York Intellectuals* (1987), and Alan Wald's *The New York Intellectuals* (1987). In each case, the scholarly footnotes are longer than Howe's original essay; what Howe saw as a loose arrangement of kindred spirits – more given to combativeness than to camaraderie – has, in retrospect, become our side of the Atlantic's Bloomsbury Circle.

However, what these scholarly studies, valuable as they are in many respects, tend to overlook is the sheer volume of fear that was an inheritance from immigrant Jewish fathers, and that often masqueraded as bravado – or as chutzpah – in the most utopian schemes of their sons. As Howe said, again in retrospect and with an understanding he would not have been able to articulate in the mid-1930s:

Immigrant Jewish life left us with a large weight of fear. Fear had seeped into Jewish bones over the centuries, fear had become the intuitive Jewish response to authority, fear seemed the strongest emotion that the very world itself, earth, sky, and sun, brought out in Jews. To be Jewish meant – not this alone, but this always – to live with fear, on the edge of foreseen catastrophe. "A Jew's joy," says the Yiddish proverb, "is not without fright."

Later, when Howe writes about the titanic struggle between Left and Right as it was so advertised during the Spanish Civil War, he sees the nightmare of our century against a backdrop of catastrophe: "Nothing else [Howe asserts somberly] reveals so graphically the tragic character of those years than that the yearning for some better world should repeatedly end in muck, foul play, murder." If history has taught us anything it is to distrust those with a programatic reading of history – whether it comes as garden variety utopianism or with a full head of Marxist steam.

And yet, for all the hard lessons of experience – the disappointments, the friends lost in the heat of critical debate, the battering that our century has given to dreams of a "world more attractive" – Howe continues to operate on what his autobiography calls "a margin of hope." *All* utopian visions are not the work of villains and thugs:

. . . surely there is another utopia. It exists at no point in time and space, it is never merely given, it cannot be willed either into existence or out of sight, it speaks for our sense of what yet may be. Or may not. But whether a real option or mere fantasy, this utopia is as needed by mankind as bread and shelter.

Dissent – the journal Howe founded in 1954, and that he has edited ever since – is, Howe tells me, both an attempt to "salvage" (that word again) what may be left of socialism and an effort to "build a bridge" toward some new, as yet unformed, political consciousness. Writing in *Commentary*, Midge Decter makes it clear that she has her doubts. Those unwilling, or constitutionally unable, to see the handwriting on the boardroom walls are destined to dream away their lives on the sidelines:

> From this [utopian] posture, no failure of policy ever need be confronted, no error need be confessed . . . he [Howe] can cling to his belief in the principles of liberty and his hopes for a worldwide movement in the public welfare without having to involve himself in the question of how those beliefs and hopes might actually be secured.

But even a book like *Socialism and America* (1985) which patiently and thoughtfully tries to explain why Socialist movements wax at some moments, wane at others – and more important, which deals with what one chapter takes up under the heading "Why has Socialism Failed in America" – contains as much hopefulness as it does elegy. In short, one wonders if those like Midge Dector have quite the stranglehold on realpolitik they so proudly claim.

By contrast, Alan Wald's book, *The New York Intellectuals* (1987) (which argues on behalf of a revitalized Trotskyism), adds yet another reductive label to those that Howe had accumulated over the span of four decades. He is an "inveterate reformer," one who insists on "proposing political solutions" that, in Wald's view, "probably assisted the decline if not the demise of the anti-Stalinist left." In a word, Howe not only began to talk about himself as a "democratic socialist," but worse, much worse, he also began to imagine that "a movement in America might choose to drop the socialist label: who needs, once again, to explain that we do *not* want the kinds of society that exist in Russia and China, Poland and Cuba? But, at least with regard to America, we continue to speak of small groups trying to keep alive a tradition."

"Trying to keep alive a tradition" – that, as much as anything, might do rough justice to the seemingly disparate activities that make up the zigzagging graph of Howe's career. Sometimes, as in *The American Newness* (1986), he appears to come full circle, returning to consider an Emerson that he had largely avoided. Writers like Hawthorne, like Melville, even like Fitzgerald, had seemed to be kindred spirits – storytellers a generation or two removed from some former, forever-lost greatness. But the transcendentally inclined Emerson was neither Howe's cup of tea nor was he his secret sharer. Still, "to confront American culture" [Howe argues] "is to feel oneself encircled by a thin but strong presence. I call it Emersonian. . . ."

Moreover, what he calls Emerson's "newness" – largely a muscular sense of the American Self at the very threshold of revolutionary possibility and freewheeling thought – permeates our literary culture and, more important, the very air we breathe, the sky under which we, as Americans, stand. To be sure, with Emerson there is much to quarrel about: the gauzy side of this thought; the easy pantheism that ends with a god in every tree; and, perhaps most of all, his habit of seeing history through a glass lightly.

Howe is right, of course, in thinking about Emerson as a spirit to which one responds – and it is in what he calls "the literature of loss" (virtually all post–Civil War writers) that he plants *his* critical feet on congenial ground. For it is loss, and what can be salvaged from that loss – the inclination toward elegy always balanced by slim, but precious margins of hope – that characterizes Howe's achievement as a critic, as a writer, as a political theorist, and as a person.

In an age where fashion exerts a grip as powerful as it is fleeting, where critics jump ship before they have sailed beyond safe, public harbors, Irving Howe is a study in what can be gained by what the title of one of his books calls "steady work." In this regard, as in so many others, his own words say what needs to be said with conviction and with eloquence:

> . . . American intellectuals seem capable of almost anything except the ultimate grace of a career devoted to some large principle or value, modulated by experience and thought, but firm in purpose.

Irving Howe has proved capable of precisely this "ultimate grace of a career," and he has done so – painfully, honestly, insightfully – in rich measure.

Getting through the Eighties

We have long assumed that novels provide the fullest, most revealing indicators of the Zeitgeist. This assumption, like so many others that used to come with the territory of literary criticism, is now very much open to question. Indeed, it may well be that with certain notable exceptions – Henry James, William Faulkner – American novelists will never surpass the extraordinary achievements of their nineteenth-century predecessors. This sobering possibility looms ever more likely as we realize how culturally thin, how personally circumscribed most serious contemporary American fiction in fact is. Minimalism is a way not only of describing a subgenre but also of pointing toward a general cultural condition.

"Gestures of Indefinite Revolt: College Life through Fictional Prisms" focuses on one aspect of the problem – young writers writing about the young; as it moves from F. Scott Fitzgerald (*This Side of Paradise*) through J. D. Salinger ("Franny") and finally to Brett Easton Ellis (*Rules of Attraction*) one can see not only the arc of decline but also something of the condition that pertains in the one world – namely, academe – where fiction is, presumably, taken seriously. By contrast, the essays on the careers of Philip Roth and Saul Bellow are designed to give one a measure of heart – partly because these authors have been with us, novel after novel, for so long and partly because their work continues to take on significant issues.

The essays in this section end with a consideration of intellectual life in America, one prompted in large part by Paul Johnson's 1988 diatribe, *Intellectuals*. If his gloomy assessment is occasioned by showing, in case study after case study, that intellectuals tend to care more about humanity in general than about individual persons, and that they care most deeply of all about their careers, their self-aggrandizement, and their pocketbooks, this hardly constitutes shocking news. That all of Johnson's intellectual villains are positioned somewhere on the Left is, of course, part of his neoconservative agenda, but his central point would not be much enhanced had he added an Ezra Pound or T. S. Eliot for every Karl Marx and Bertrand Russell.

Indeed, if one has a taste for conspiratorial theories, the cause of America's declining intellectual life might be better laid at the doorsteps of our colleges and universities. Being an intellectual — which is to say, a specialist at being a nonspecialist, and one whose essays take on large cultural subjects in plain, jargon-free English — butters very few academic parsnips. In short, we have come very far from the cultural world in which a Philip Rahv could speculate widely about palefaces and redskins. His name reappears in "Revisionist Thought, Academic Power, and the Aging American Intellectual" as a reminder, perhaps even as an inspiration, but certainly as a way of bringing my general argument, and the essays of this collection, full circle.

Gestures of
Indefinite Revolt:
College Life through
Fictional Prisms

Here was a new generation, shouting
the old cries, learning the old creeds,
through a revery of long days and
nights; . . . grown up to find all Gods
dead, all wars fought, all faiths in
man shaken. . . .
from F. Scott Fitzgerald's *This Side of*
Paradise

Irving Howe's intellectual memoir, *A Margin of Hope* (1982), is, among other things, an account of his days as a student activist at New York's City College. By the usual academic standards he was, let us say, a marginal student: "I'd go to class, sit impatiently for a few minutes until the roll was called, slip out, head for the lunchroom where a political argument was waiting, and at the hour's end race back to get the books I had left in the classroom." For Howe, the real action at City College took place not in its lecture halls, but in the fabled Alcove 1 where his fellow Trotskyites took on the Young Communists who held down the fort at an equally fabled Alcove 2. Howe's comrades may have been outnumbered (the Young Communist League could boast of some 400 members, while the combative, anti-Stalinist Left barely numbered 50), but they were – at least as *he* remembers it – never verbally outgunned.

So much has been written recently about the life and times of the New York Jewish intellectual crowd one might well conclude that *everyone* in City College's Class of 1940 was passionate, combative, and committed to radical politics. The facts of the matter, as Howe himself points out, suggest otherwise:

And where, meanwhile, were the twenty thousand students of City College? Some, utterly indifferent to radical or any other politics, kept faithful to their studies, perhaps hoping for a better future than seemed probable at the time. Some juggled an array of part-time jobs in order to keep going to school, though why they wanted to keep going was not always clear. Some were hopeless careerists (especially, we thought, the engineers), determined at any cost to "make it." . . . As always, the politically active students formed a minority. . . .

Howe's savvy remarks serve not only as a corrective to nostalgic accounts of "how it was" during the 1930s, but his insights about the many and the few can also stand as a cautionary tale when the focus shifts to wider discussions of college life and ways it is represented in fiction. There are works, after all, that reflect college life and those that tend to *shape* it, those that chronicle the prevailing sociological trends and those that strike us as more prophetic, as more lasting, and as more important. The differences are what this essay seeks to explore.

As Edmund Wilson's exquisitely cadenced words would have it, *This Side of Paradise* is "really not *about* anything: its intellectual and moral content amounts to little more than a gesture – a gesture of indefinite revolt." Granted, the "gestures" have changed since the days when Fitzgerald described Princeton as "the pleasantest country club in America," but I would argue that "indefinite revolt" remains the central condition and the dominant shape of our most interesting fictions about college life.

In the case of *This Side of Paradise*, Fitzgerald may have grabbed hold of a hotter wire than he realized, for despite what Wilson saw as its glaring deficiencies – its "bogus ideas and faked literary references," its "literary words tossed about with the most reckless inaccuracy," its appalling number of misspellings and solecisms – the novel *lived* for Wilson and continues to live for college students whose lives differ significantly from that of Fitzgerald's protagonist, Amory Blaine. There are reasons why this should not be so. To find out about "petting shirts," for example, contemporary students must go to the library in search of information as dated as Amory's moral code: he "found it rather fascinating to feel that any popular girl he met before eight he might quite possibly kiss before twelve." In sexual matters, the ante has gone up considerably; exploits that seemed risqué in 1900 look quaint and tame from today's perspective, when a burning issue on many campuses concerns whether the administration should provide free condoms to its students or if it is merely required to install condom dispensers in all the dormitories.

What seems to endure from Fitzgerald's generation down to our own are Amory's "gestures of indefinite revolt" – for example, his sense of uncertainty about what he calls "the next thing." On Amory's lips the phrase strikes one as impossibly vague, but Monsignor Darcy (the priest who represents mature understanding in the novel) argues that the challenge of whatever might come next is inextricably tied to the distinction between having a personality and being a personage:

> Personality is a physical matter almost entirely; it lowers the people it acts on – I've seen it vanish in a long sickness. But while a personality is active, it overrides "the next thing." Now a personage, on the other hand, gathers. He is never thought of apart from what he'd done. He's a bar on which a thousand things have been hung – glittering things sometimes, as ours are, but he uses those things with a cold mentality back of them.

Amory is a sucker for big ideas, and much of the novel is devoted to his efforts to try on the cape, and the postures, of various roles: big man on campus, romantic poet, ersatz socialist. At the same time, of course, he is both attracted to and repulsed by the loud, undergraduate rhythms that swirl around him. In short, Amory's sense of self is continually "in riot," and it is precisely this uncertain sense of how to respond to competing, even contradictory claims on his allegiance that students respond to in *This Side of Paradise*. Like Amory, today's students find that confusion comes with the undergraduate territory; however, what they often fail to recognize is the artistic patterning that distinguishes Fitzgerald's novel.

For Amory – and to an extent for Fitzgerald as well – all of life's roads lead back to Princeton. Its "glittering caste system" never lost its shine, even though all the usual ways of becoming a "top cat" – by scoring the winning touchdown at the Princeton-Harvard game, by joining the best club, by deciding the songs they'd sing at Triangle productions and the poems they'd publish at the Nassau Lit, or by strolling into the prom with a beautiful girl on your arm – managed to elude him. Given all this, it is hardly surprising that Theodore Roethke, who thought himself a tougher cookie, wrote Fitzgerald down as one who was "born and died a Princeton sophomore."

Later, of course, Fitzgerald would add his name to the list of American authors destroyed by booze and women, but at Princeton it was molecules, calculus, and irregular verbs that did him in. Even this academic revolt has its indefinite aspect in the novel, as we see in Amory's romantic revery on the scholarly life and academic architecture:

> The towers that in view of his window sprang upward, grew into a spire, yearning higher until its uppermost tip was half invisible against the morning skies, gave him the first sense of the transiency and unimportance of the campus figures except as holders of the apostolic succession. He liked knowing that Gothic architecture, with its upward trend, was peculiarly appropriate to universities, and the idea became personal to him. The silent stretches of green, the quiet halls with an occasional late-burning scholastic light held his imagination in a strong grasp, and the chastity of the spire became a symbol of this perception.

"Damn it all," he whispered aloud, wetting his hands in the damp and running them through his hair. "Next year I work!"

In Amory's case, however, resolutions are easier to make than to carry through, and this is especially so when they pit hard work against daydream. Then, as now, genuine learning required the discipline, the *sitzfleish*, if you will, to solve a series of discreet intellectual challenges, to master one specific text after another. However much Amory Blaine might yearn to make his mark as a scholar, he is primarily concerned about making a public splash. In his case, gesture – rather than ripeness – is all. Consider, for example, the scene in which Amory turns a fateful letter from the Registrar's office into the stuff of melodrama. If the slip turns out to be pink, he has passed the requisite number of courses and can retain his position on the editorial board of the *Princetonian*; however, if the slip is blue, he will join the ranks of those sensitive souls who have also crashed on the rocks of academe:

> "Watch my face, gentlemen, for the primitive emotions."
> He tore it open and held the slip up to the light.
> "Well?"
> "Pink or blue?"
> "Say what it is."
> "We're all ears, Amory."
> "Smile or swear – or something."
> There was a pause. . . . a small crowd of seconds swept by. . . . then he looked again and another crowd went on into time.
> "Blue as the sky, gentlemen."

The bravado of the moment is nearly as delicious, as romantic, as the painful memories that cluster predictably around Amory's defeat. Once again, Monsignor Darcy has pegged him early – and with a deadly accuracy – as a collector of lost causes whether they be attached to Hannibal or Bonnie Prince Charlie, the Southern Confederacy or the tragic sweep of Irish history. Most of all, however, Amory enjoys the specialness that only youthful disappointments can confer. Unlike raccoon coats and the Charleston, self-indulgence seems always in style on college campuses, particularly among those who make a career of collecting evidence that they have been misunderstood – by their teachers, their classmates, their girl- or boyfriends, indeed by the universe itself.

Much has been made of the revisions that transmogrified sections of Fitzgerald's undergraduate notebook, scenes from Triangle Club plays, and drafts of *The Romantic Egotist* into *This Side of Paradise* (see, for example, James West's *The Making of This Side of Paradise*, 1983); and even more has been written about how the novel's extraordinary success made the marriage of Scott and Zelda, our century's most enduring star-crossed lovers, possible, but what is often overlooked is the way that the novel's "indefinite" themes, its mishmash of attitudes and postures, take on an archetypal dimension for college readers. Fitzgerald designed *This Side of Paradise* to join other "quest books" – principally, Compton Mackenzie's *Sinister Street* (1913–1914) – as a chronicle of the discovered self. Despite his ego-shattering blue slip, despite the fact that he will leave Princeton sans degree, Amory insists that he has "managed to pick up a good education," and that whatever he may *not* know, "the water of disillusions had left a deposit on his soul, responsibility and love of life, the faint stirring of old ambitions and unrealized dreams." No doubt E. D. Hirsch, the author of *Cultural Literacy* (1987), would prefer an Amory who could recognize terms such as "isosceles triangle" and "Trojan horse" when he saw them. Amory, of course, dreams about bigger, more transcendental fish. Like Gatsby, he stretches out his arms – not, to be sure, toward the green dock light that signifies Daisy but in breathless anticipation of "the crystalline, radiant sky." As his final, operatic outburst would have it: "I know myself."

One need not number oneself among the E. D. Hirsches, the William Bennetts, the Allan Blooms, to smile and gently point out that Amory's declaration has a hollow, unsubstantiated ring, but who among us would not prefer his pretentions to the passive, note-taking types we meet in our classrooms today? For if Fitzgerald, like his mouthpiece, Amory, belongs to a generation that could no longer believe in smug, Victorian values, he also is part of an age struggling to write its own etiquette book. With the possible exception of Christian Gauss, none of the learned professors of Princeton seemed aware that a literary revolution, one we now know as literary modernism, was taking place beneath their very noses. Had Fitzgerald gone to college a few years earlier and had he attended the University of Pennsylvania rather than Princeton, he might have run into an Ezra Pound, a William Carlos Williams, a Hilda Doolittle. Not that Fitzgerald lacked for distinguished literary company: there was, after all, John Peale Bishop (the model for Thomas Parke D'Invilliers, poet extraordinaire) and, most importantly, Edmund Wilson. But what Fitzgerald, the novelist, lacked were the appropriate *forms* for his rebellious content. These would come later, in the lessons he learned from Ernest Hemingway, James Joyce, Gertrude Stein, and John Dos Passos.

Some thirty years after Amory "sought among the lights of Princeton for some one who might found the Great American Poetic Tradition," J. D. Salinger's Franny Glass arrived for a Princeton football weekend clutching a well-thumbed copy of *The Way of a Pilgrim* and pondering her own "gestures of indefinite revolt." Her date, Lane Coutell, is a study in what "The Age of Criticism" has wrought, in what literature has come to mean among Princeton's brighter, more ambitious undergraduates:

> "I mean, to put it crudely . . . the thing he [Flaubert] lacks is testicularity. Know what I mean? . . . Anyway, that was the motif of the thing, so to speak — what I was trying to bring out in a fairly subtle way. . . . I mean, God. I honestly thought it was going to go over like a goddam lead balloon, and when I got it back with this goddam 'A' on it in a letter almost six foot high, I swear I almost keeled over."

Lane dresses, smokes, and — most of all — *talks* in the requisite Salinger 1950s mode. He is, in short, a portrait of Ivy League conformity, one as ingratiating as it is transparent. Holden Caulfield had a word for Coutell's type: "flit"; and Ian Hamilton's recent effort at biography, *In Search of J. D. Salinger* (1988), makes it clear that Salinger himself never quite recovered from his days as an undergraduate Ivy-basher.

Franny teeters on the nervous edge of breakdown where others in the Glass family have established something akin to squatter's rights. If Holden divides the world – neatly, arbitrarily, desperately – into the many who are phony and the precious few who are authentic, Franny aims her discontent at all that is "tiny and meaningless and – sad-making." In a word, at everything dominated by *ego*: "I'm just sick of ego, ego, ego. My own and everybody else's. I'm sick of everybody that wants to *get* somewhere, do something distinguished and all, be somebody interesting. It's disgusting – it is, it *is*. I don't care what anybody says." For Franny, mysticism – as exemplified by *The Way of a Pilgrim* – not only counters the "tearer-downers" known as "section-men" but also replaces the self with the body's capacity to pray incessantly. As she tries to explain this concept to Lane:

> "Well, as I said, the pilgrim – this simple peasant – started the whole pilgrimage to find out what it means in the Bible when it says you're supposed to pray without ceasing. . . . the starets [according to Franny, 'a very advanced religious person'] tells him about the Jesus Prayer first of all. 'Lord Jesus Christ, have mercy on me.' . . . Anyway, the starets tells the pilgrim that if you keep saying that prayer over and over again – you only have to just do it with your lips at first – then eventually what happens, the prayer becomes self-active. Something *happens* after a while. I don't know what, but something happens, and the words get synchronized with the person's heartbeats, and then you're actually praying without ceasing. Which has a really tremendous mystical effect on your whole outlook. I mean that's the whole *point* of it, more or less. I mean you do it to purify your whole outlook and get an absolutely new conception of what everything's about."

Lane, of course, is too absorbed in his Flaubert paper to hear. "This guy Brughman thinks I ought to publish the goddam paper somewhere," he tells Franny with as much matter-of-factness as he can muster. Presumably, he'll *think* about it (as if he had been thinking about anything else!), but as he puts it, doing his best to feign a sophisticated indifference: "I don't know, though." After

all, "'. . . critical essays on Flaubert and those boys are a goddam
dime a dozen. . . . [Still] I don't think there've been any really
in*cis*ive jobs done on him in the last –'"

Indeed, Salinger piles one undercutting detail upon another until Lane Coutell's facade comes tumbling down and he is revealed
as the pompous, affected young bore he clearly is. Prick him and
he bleeds Big Ideas onto erasable bond:

> "I mean the emphasis I put on *why* he was so neurotically at-
> tracted to the *mot juste* wasn't too bad. I mean in the light of
> what we know today. Not just psychoanalysis and all that
> crap, but certainly to a certain extent. You know what I mean.
> I'm no Freudian man or anything like that, but certain things
> you can't just pass over as capital-F Freudian and let them go
> at that. I mean to a certain extent I think I was perfectly justi-
> fied to point out that none of the really good boys – Tolstoy,
> Dostoevski, *Shakespeare*, for Chrissake – were such goddam
> word-squeezers."

By contrast, Franny's deepest anxiety is not that she's afraid of
competing, but rather that she will compete all too well, that she
will become a version of Lane:

> "That's why I quit the Theatre Department. Just because I'm
> so horribly conditioned to accept everybody else's values, and
> just because I like applause and people to rave about me,
> doesn't make it right. I'm ashamed of it. I'm sick of it. I'm
> sick of not having the courage to be an absolute nobody."

Apparently Salinger himself has brooded long and hard over similar anxieties, as everything from Holden's remarks about Ernie, the
Village piano player who wows his audiences with fluff instead of
art, to Salinger's own decision not to publish any of his fiction after
"Hapworth 16, 1924" (1965) testifies.

To such sentiments Fitzgerald could have only shaken his head
in disbelief. The glitter of public life drew him in ways that were as
complicated as they were ultimately tragic. In his best work he was
simultaneously the Jazz Age's most perceptive chronicler and its
sharpest moral critic, and even if one grants that the formula is

muddled in *This Side of Paradise*, one nonetheless feels that there are moments when aesthetic distance and ironic detachment count for more than self-pity. In the 1950s, however, the private self, pure and unadulterated, mattered above all else, especially when its cult heroes ventured forth to attack what the next generation would call the Establishment. Manlius and Esposito – poets who teach at Franny's college – are a case in point. As Franny insists, "they're not *real* poets," but merely "people that write poems that get published and anthologized all over the place." To be a *real* poet – that is, Franny's kind of poet, and if the evidence in the Hamilton biography be accurate, Salinger's as well – one must ". . . do something beautiful. I mean you're supposed to *leave* something beautiful after you get off the page and everything. The ones you're talking about don't leave a single, solitary thing beautiful." To make matters worse, what the likes of Manlius and Esposito do leave behind are little more than "terribly fascinating, syntax droppings" – the grist that section-men will one day turn into scholarly articles.

And so, between her chicken sandwich and Lane's nonstop monologue falls the shadow of Franny's deepening spiritual/emotional crisis. For better or worse, the Franny who bonked competition on the beezer came to stand for sensitivity incarnate, for the inchoate revolt of an entire generation. Small wonder, then, that copies of *The Way of a Pilgrim* began cropping up in undergraduate bookbags. Granted, *The Catcher in the Rye* has had a longer run as a how-to book of significant gestures, but I would argue that aspects of "Franny" – principally its exploration of College Life and its Discontents – transcend Franny's time and Lane's place.

Salinger, of course, writes about the young with equal amounts of sympathy and distance. The latter cannot be said of Brett Easton Ellis. He was still a Bennington College undergraduate when his first novel, *Less Than Zero* (1985) turned him into a cause célèbre. No matter that literary critics calculated his "grade" in negative numbers; no matter that those who know better winced when his account of life in L.A.'s fast lane was compared to *This Side of Paradise*, to *The Sun Also Rises*, to *On the Road*, and, predictably enough, to *The Catcher in the Rye*. *Less Than Zero* moved effortlessly from its first blush as a bad book to its incarnation as a wretched film without so much as skipping a beat, and Ellis himself became a "literary personality" – a writer known for being known.

The Rules of Attraction (1987) is another installment from Ellis's "no-sweat" school of sociological fiction. After all, the argument goes, who knows the real scoop about college life – about the designer drugs and endless drinking parties, about the brand names students wear and drive, about the "in" music and the enormous variety of casual sex – better than a recent graduate willing to tell the sordid truth? For writers such as Ann Beattie and Bobbie Ann Mason the texture of pop references (e.g., brand names, current films, and top-forty ditties) is the stuff of K Mart realism; by contrast, Ellis casts *his* eyes on the welter of sociological detail that surrounds students at our more exclusive and considerably more expensive private colleges. One response, of course, is to argue that Ellis's long suit is fanciful, ultimately exploitive exaggeration rather than reportage; another is to take him seriously and vow never to send a son or daughter to Bennington, the model for Ellis's fictional Camden College.

I prefer to let my friends in the social sciences debate the accuracy of Ellis's vision with any hard evidence they can muster; as a literary critic, I am convinced by his paragraphs that *The Rules of Attraction* is thin, unconvincing fare:

CLAY   People are afraid to walk across campus after midnight. Someone on acid whispers this to me, one Sunday dawn after I have been up on crystal meth most of the week crying, and I know it is true. This person is in my computer class (which is now my major) and I see him in the weight room and sometimes I see him at the municipal pool on Main Street, in town. A place I spend what some people think is an inordinate amount of time. (They also have a good tanning salon next door.) I keep my Walkman on a lot this term, listening to groups that have broken up: The Eagles, the Doors, the Go-Go's. . . .

I go to an Elvis Costello concert in New York but get lost on the way back to Camden. I cannot get cable to hook up MTV in my dorm room so I buy a VCR and get videos in a cheap video rental store in town. I buy a Porsche, second-hand, in New York before the term starts so I have a car to do these things. People are also afraid to eat sushi in New Hampshire.

In Clay's version of the Cartesian equation, people are what they buy. Unfortunately, this insistence is widespread at Camden College, and the result makes it hard to keep the novel's various "speakers" straight: each of them holds forth in short bursts, and each sounds precisely like the others. In short, the students who attend Camden College are rich and spoiled, bored and boring. Once again, the Fitzgerald who took such pains to populate *This Side of Paradise* with representative, yet individualized, "types" would hardly be amused by the conformity that lies just beneath the veneer of Ellis's gestures of undergraduate revolt. For one thing, Ellis's "gestures" are both defiant and predictable, full of self-righteous justification rather than confusion.

To be sure, *fashion* is a goodly part of the novel's appeal. As its opening salvo puts it:

> and it's a story that might bore you but you don't have to listen, she told me, because she always knew it was going to be like that, and it was, she thinks, her first year, or, actually weekend, really a Friday, in September, at Camden, and this was three or four years ago, and she got so drunk that she ended up in bed, lost her virginity (late, she was eighteen) in Lorna Slavin's room, because she was a Freshman and had a roommate sometimes at her boyfriend's place off-campus, who she thought was a Sophomore Ceramics major but who was actually either some guy from N.Y.U., a film student, and up in New Hampshire just for the Dressed to Get Screwed Party, or a townie.

In an age not formed by MTV and other cultural junk food such writing might have tried to pass itself off as stream-of-consciousness, but there is precious little "consciousness" in Ellis's world. His students are either bombed on booze or zonked on drugs – and never more so than when they flop into the sack. In *The Rules of*

Attraction, a one-night stand qualifies as a stable relationship; the more common situation at Camden is frenetic, desperate, and decidedly shorter.

But if words such as "purpose" or "value" have lost all meaning in the fog that is Camden College life, sheer variety has also become a casualty. In short, Ellis's students strike me as interchangeable parts. They major in 1980s chic, and it is here – rather than in the classroom – where one's GPA counts. Wear the wrong clothes, talk the wrong talk – in a phrase, fail to conform – and you are sure to be shunned, which, at Camden, is likely to mean that you'll have to watch *Texas Chainsaw Massacre* all alone.

Indeed, at one point in the novel a group of characters comes up with a collective list of *outré* behavior – grounds for banishment – that includes anybody who (1) smokes clove cigarettes, (2) writes poetry about womanhood, (3) considers himself born again, (4) returns from a semester in London with a British accent, (5) comes to breakfast after a night's sleep, (6) waits to get braces until after high school, (7) has parents who are still married. I can hear Ellis's defenders muttering that I have missed the joke, that I am taking this meaningless talk much, much too seriously. Perhaps, but I would point out that *The Rules of Attraction* is more than two hundred pages of exactly such meaningless talk. Here, for example, is a slice of typical "party" chatter:

> I would ask her if she'd ever read Hemingway. (I don't know why I asked her about him since I never had read that much.) She would tell me about Allen Ginsberg and Gertrude Stein and Joan Baez. I asked her if she had read *Howl* (which I had only heard about through some crazy class called Poetry and the Fifties, which I failed) and she said, "No. Sounds harsh."

Given the choice of having lunch with any of Ellis's characters or being stuck in an elevator with someone selling insurance, I would opt happily for the latter. And the same thing holds true if I were offered a choice between reading virtually any of Ellis's paragraphs or the fine print at the bottom of my homeowner's policy. Legalese in nine-point type is no fun, but neither is this run of self-indulgence passing itself off as fiction:

PAUL   Then I find myself wandering down College Drive approaching Wooley House, where the Dressed to Get Screwed party was. The campus is dead, unawake, even though it's almost noon, which means they will have all missed brunch, and I smile with satisfaction at the knowledge of this luxury withheld from them. All the windows have been smashed at Wooley, ripped sheets lay rolled up in balls all over the green lawn outside the broken French windows of the living room, or hang from trees like big deflated balloons. Flies buzz around three sticky trashcans that are lying on their sides in the cool autumn sun, drying. There are three people asleep, or dead, two of them sitting up, in the living room, one of them naked, face-down. Vomit, beer, wine, cigarette smoke, punch, marijuana, even the smell of sex, semen, sweat, women permeate the room, hang in the air like haze.

It is possible, of course, that Ellis takes his media image seriously, that he sees his burned-out, fin de siècle prose as the best way to capture a jaded, burned-out college generation. Given enough ingenuity, even cynicism and self-destructive behavior can be counted among the "gestures of indefinite revolt." But I suspect that Ellis is laughing all the way to Elaine's. After all, *The Rules of Attraction* will keep him in Italian knits and Elvis Costello tapes for a long time. Ellis apparently makes it a point of honor to put the kibosh on his own revisions and on any editing by others. That kind of literature is for the geeks who went to class and plowed through the Norton anthologies. Reading his novels one feels reasonably sure that Ellis has studiously avoided both conditions, and even more confident that reading itself counts for precious little in the world of his fiction. That was decidedly *not* the case with Amory Blaine or even, in her own way, with Franny Glass.

What, then, does this admittedly selective triad of *This Side of Paradise*, "Franny," and *The Rules of Attraction* tell us about literature's capacity to deal with college life, and vice versa? Surely one might argue that Owen Johnson's *Stover at Yale* (1912) was as widely read – and in its own way, was as influential – as *This Side of Paradise*; or that the Eugene Grant of Thomas Wolfe's *Of Time and the*

River (1935) is at least as sensitive and as out-of-place at Harvard as Franny is at her Princeton weekend. As an early study such as John O. Lyons's *The College Novel in America* (1962) argues, "There is no end to the portraits of undergraduates that have appeared between hard covers," especially if one includes academic satires in the tally. (Lyons's bibliography includes in excess of 250 items, ranging from Nathaniel Hawthorne's *Fanshawe* [1828] to Louis Simpson's *Riverside Drive* [1962].) But that much said by way of giving a subgenre its due, the plain truth is that academic life is nearly incidental to our most memorable "academic novels": Mary McCarthy's *The Groves of Academe* (1952) or Randall Jarrell's *Pictures from an Institution* (1954), Bernard Malamud's *A New Life* (1961) or Vladimir Nabokov's *Pale Fire* (1962). Provide *too* much realism, too many accounts of themes assigned and graded, of faculty meetings and office conferences, and the result is a species of sociology – perhaps interesting to academics (who relax with yet another tale of Eyesore U. in the way that others read detective stories or bodice-rippers), but hardly fiction of the first rank. In this sense, a novel such as Alan Lelchuk's *American Mischief* (1973) – an account of "how it was" during the troubled times of the late 1960s – is a sure bet to join Anna Ray's *Ackroyd of the Faculty* (1907) and Percy Marks's *The Plastic Age* (1924) in the ranks of forgotten academic novels. Only Brits like C. P. Snow (*The Masters*, 1960) and David Lodge (*Changing Places* [1975], *Small World* [1984], *Nice Work* [1988], et al.) seem able to write about academe with the wit and the insight that the form requires.

And yet, whatever the shortcomings of *This Side of Paradise*, "Franny," and *The Rules of Attraction*, these works tell us much – indeed, sometimes much more than we would like to know – about the lives that college students actually live in dormitories and fraternity houses. It should come as no great surprise that capital-L Literature counts for less than it did in Fitzgerald's day, but I would submit that there is knowing, and *knowing*. To be sure, Franny can be brushed aside as one of Salinger's marvelous eccentrics, and therefore a special case. With Ellis's characters one is less confident. During the worst moments of the 1960s Richard Hofstadter imagined writing a study of America entitled "The Age of Garbage"; were he alive today he would, no doubt, want to revise his title. "Son of Shlock" has a nice ring to it, one that suggests a certain continuity of cultural thinness. On second thought, however, I suspect that Hofstadter would prefer "Schlock IV," relishing not only the play on how Hollywood merchandises its junk but also the nice irony that, at last, an entire generation – including the most zonked-out character in *The Rules of Attraction* – could recognize the roman numerals.

Deconstruction as Apology:
The Counterfictions of
Philip Roth

Let's face it, even the worst criticism
contains some truth. They always see
something you're trying to hide.
Nathan Zuckerman

I f it is true that literary modernists such as Joyce, Kafka, and Chekov continue to cast their long, unrelenting shadows over Philip Roth's work, it is also true that his congenial themes and characteristic techniques have taken an increasingly postmodernist turn. In the beginning, there was the narrative word, the voice that arranged, say, the fateful meetings between Neil Klugman and Brenda Patamkin or the psychological warfare between Sergeant Marx and the goldbricking Grossbart. To be sure, that voice packed a *tone* and a wallop – especially for those readers of *Goodbye, Columbus* (1959) who preferred to see American Jews paraded through the public print with more dignity, more decorum. Roth's Jews may have been familiar types, but that was precisely the point: literature, the offended argued, ought to provide models of excellence, and all the more so if the American-Jewish suburbs were going through a bad meretricious patch.

What Roth saw, of course, was the possibility of liberating himself from the tribal fears that were his immigrant Jewish legacy. As he explains in *Reading Myself and Others* (1975), *his* book of self-conscious explanation:

I was strongly influenced by a sit-down comic named Franz Kafka and a very funny bit he does called "The Metamorphosis." . . . not until I had got hold of guilt, you see, as a comic idea, did I begin to feel myself lifting free and clear of my last book and my old concerns.

What Roth *doesn't* tell us – indeed, what he could not have realized at the time – is just how long, how protracted, and finally how impossible this struggle was likely to be. Whatever else *Portnoy's Complaint* (1969) may be in terms of an effort – at once desperate and heroic, foolhardy and comic – to *enjoy* being bad, the novel itself is all prolegomenon. The proudest boast of Whitman's persona is that he chants his "barbaric yawp" over the rooftops of the world – untranslatable, unique, and forever unavailable to those who prefer their poetry polite and neatly captured on the page. Touch *these* "leaves," he insists, and you have touched a man! By contrast, Alexander Portnoy is the crown prince of whiners, a man with enough *tsoris* to beat all-comers in a misery contest. Roth, I would argue, never quite recovered from the "surprises" (as he called them) that the extraordinary success of *Portnoy's Complaint* brought. Granted, he had never set himself up as a patient Griselda, and even in the "old days" – that is, the days before a Jacqueline Susann could crack up the "Tonight Show" crowd by telling Johnny Carson that she thought Roth was a good writer, but that she preferred not to shake hands with him – he tried to silence his critics by writing essays full of explanatory sound and justifying fury. However, from *My Life as a Man* (1974) onward, Roth's novels began to glance uneasily over their shoulders at who, or what, might be gaining on them; and perhaps more important, they became increasingly self-conscious about the very act of writing fiction and about fictionality itself. Roth himself seemed divided between contradictory images of the author – one, as the schlemiel who has caused his own misfortunes; the other as the nice, hardworking Jewish boy who should not be confused with his *meshuganah* (crazy) protagonists.

In *Portnoy's Complaint*, Alexander *kvetches*, and then *kvetches* some more – all with the hope that "*kvetching* for me [might be] a form of truth." With *My Life as a Man*, Peter Tarnopol tells his story, and tells it, and *tells* it – all in the desperate hope that he will one day see the figure in his carpet, that the disparate pieces of his abortive marriage will fall, magically, into an aesthetic whole and at last make sense. To that end, he creates Nathan Zuckerman, a countervoice who provides the distancing that art requires. Of Zuckerman we will hear much – indeed, sometimes more than we would prefer – but Tarnopol disappears, apparently forever, with *My Life as a Man*'s final page.

The effect, of course, is the familiar modernist device of stories-within-stories, or a reflexivity that turns the House of Fiction into a hall of mirrors. But that said, Roth adds a deconstructive note to the proceedings, one that may have been sounded before, but never, I would submit, so stridently or so systematically. For example, there is a moment in Joyce's *A Portrait of the Artist as a Young Man* (1916) in which the young Stephen Dedalus imagines his villanelle being "read out at breakfast amid the tapping of egg-shells"; such is the callous treatment that serious writers can expect when their work falls into the hands of philistines. By contrast, Tarnopol's "useful fictions" collect enough in-depth analysis to qualify for a Norton Critical Edition. His sister Joan suggests – rightly, I think – that he "can't make pleasure credible," while his brother Morris, a specialist in blunt, no-nonsense talk, puts it this way:

> "What is it with you Jewish writers? Madeleine Herzog, Deborah Rojak, the cutesie-pie castrator in *After the Fall*, and isn't the desirable shiksa of *A New Life* a kvetch and titless in the bargain? And now, for the further delight of the rabbis and the reading public, Lydia Zuckerman, that Gentile tomato. Chicken soup in every pot, and a Greshenka in every garage. With all the Dark Ladies to choose from, you luftmenschen can really pick 'em. Peppy, why are you still wasting your talent on that Dead End Kid? Leave her to heaven, okay?"

Indeed, the list of those with a fix on Tarnopol's stories, and on Tarnopol himself, reads like an index to the novel itself. And while it is relatively easy to dismiss, say, Dr. Speilvogel's reductively Freudian theory about the "phallic threatening mother figure" in his analysand's carpet, what is one to say of the undergraduate paper written by Karen Oakes, crackerjack close reader and ex-lover:

> In order to dilute the self-pity that (as I understand it) has poisoned his imagination in numerous attempts to fictionize his unhappy marriage, Professor Tarnopol establishes at the outset here a tone of covert (and, to some small degree, self-congratulatory) self-mockery; this calculated attitude of comic detachment he maintains right on down to the last paragraph, where abruptly the shield of lightheartedness is all at once pierced by the author's pronouncement that in his estimation the true story really isn't funny at all. All of which would appear to suggest that if Professor Tarnopol has managed in "Salad Days" to make an artful narrative of his misery, he has done so largely by refusing directly to confront it.

Such insights earn Oakes a well-deserved A+, but she is hardly alone in isolating the terms of Tarnopol's "problem" and in offering up an Rx that would cure it; the rub, of course, is that Tarnopol needs his *tsoris* and his rage if he is to keep faith with the kind of writer he is. *The Facts* (1989) confirmed what many of Roth's critics had long suspected – namely, that of all his books, *My Life as a Man* was closest to the bone:

> Probably nothing else in my work more precisely duplicates the autobiographical facts. Those scenes [in which a naive Tarnopol is duped into a disastrous marriage] represent one of the few occasions when I haven't spontaneously set out to improve on actuality in the interest of being more interesting. I couldn't have been more interesting – I couldn't have been *as* interesting. What Josie came up with, altogether on her own, was a little gem of treacherous invention, economically lurid, obvious, degrading, deluded, almost comically simple, and best of all, magically effective. . . . Without doubt she was my worst enemy ever, but, alas, she was also nothing less than the greatest creative-writing teacher of them all, specialist par excellence in the aesthetics of extremist fiction.
>
> Reader, I married her.

To ask that a Tarnopol quit harping about his psychopathic muse is rather like asking Roth to provide us with more "representative" – i.e., admirable – women rather than versions of the unbalanced, destructive creature he married.

As Amy Bellette puts it in *The Ghost Writer* (1979), the Master – E. E. Lonoff – is "counter-suggestable"; one manipulates him via reverse psychology in much the same manner that, say, Poe's cerebral detectives match their wits against master criminals. The games that result are both subtle and stylistically dazzling. To be sure, Nathan Zuckerman *dreams* many of the complications – for example, that Amy Bellette is *the* Anne Frank, an Anne Frank who survived, who "got away"; and that her extraordinary book exacts a silence, an ostensible death, in short, the shadowy life as a "ghost writer," if it is to retain its raw emotional power – but this counter-text is also an extended exercise in defending, in justifying, and, I would add, in deconstructing the knotty question of an artist's responsibility.

For Doc Zuckerman, the consequences of art are as clear, as undeniable, as the Jewish nose on Nathan's face:

> ". . . from a lifetime of experience I happen to know what ordinary people will think when they read something like this story ["Higher Education"]. And you don't. You can't. . . . But I will tell you. They don't think about how it's a great work of art. They don't know about art. . . . But that's my point. People don't read art – they read about *people*. And they judge them as such. And how do you think they will judge the people in your story, what conclusions do you think they will reach? Have you thought about that?"

The young Nathan Zuckerman, surprised by his father's surprise, hurt by his father's hurt, thinks about loftier matters: the shape and ring of individual sentences, the rise and resolution of dramatic tensions, in short, about aesthetic considerations far removed from those messy interferences that now travel under the banner of "reader response," but that, in Doc Zuckerman's Newark, boil down to the existential business of what is, or is not, good for the Jews. Read *this* way, Nathan's story strikes his father as an accident waiting to happen; it confirms, from one of their own no less and in public print to boot, what anti-Semites have long suspected — namely, that Jews squabble over money, that they are, in a word, kikes.

Small wonder, then, that Nathan seeks the "sponsorship," the surrogate fatherhood, of E. I. Lonoff. As a consummate Jewish-American fictionist, *he* will be able to extend the welcoming hand that Nathan's own father has refused. What Nathan discovers, however, is a man so committed to fantasy that the slightest hint of life has been rigorously, systematically, crowded out. "I turn sentences around," Lonoff declares. "That's my life. I write a sentence and then I turn it around. Then I look at it and I turn it around again. Then I have lunch. . . ." Although Lonoff tells his writing students that "there is no life without patience," he has little patience with the "deep thinkers" who are attracted to his work, and no doubt he would have even less patience with a deconstructive reading of his working habits.

By contrast, Zuckerman's aesthetic feeds on turbulence, on mounting tensions, on a world where sentences are shouted across a kitchen table and end in exclamation points. "You are not somebody who writes this kind of story," Doc Zuckerman insists, "and then pretends it's the truth." But Nathan *did* write such a story; moreover, he *is* precisely "the kind of person who writes this kind of story." For Lonoff, such truths are as much a part of the artistic landscape as the regimen of daily reading and obsessive scribbling. Zuckerman may be a nice polite boy when invited into somebody's home, but he is not likely to be so politic when he writes up the report of his visit. With a pen in his hand, Nathan becomes a different person, and if Lonoff's "blessing" is anywhere in the text, it is in his understanding, accepting wish that Nathan continue to be this "different person" when he sets about composing the novel we know as *The Ghost Writer*.

For those who would brand Zuckerman as self-hating, as an enemy of his people, nothing short of marrying Anne Frank will suffice. And indeed, Zuckerman imagines exactly this triumph as a logical consequence of his imaginative rescue. Not only would he who had been misunderstood now be forgiven, but his father would utter the very words Nathan most wants to hear: *"Anne, says my father – the Anne? Oh, how I have misunderstood my son. How mistaken we have been!"*

To be sure, the Anne Frank Nathan resurrects – the impassioned little sister of Kafka who lived out in Amsterdam the indictments, the hidden attics, the camouflaged doors he had dreamed about in Prague – is a psychological ringer for Nathan himself: both exact their rebellions against family, synagogue, and state in the pages of their respective works; both suffer the loss of fathers for their art; and interesting enough, *neither* could answer Judge Wapter's questions (Number 3, for example, asks: "Do you practice Judaism? If so, how? If not, what credentials qualify you for writing about Jewish life for national magazines?") in ways that he would find satisfactory.

The Ghost Writer is, of course, a version of the modernist bildungsroman as reflected through the lens of a Nathan Zuckerman some twenty years old and presumably light-years sadder-and-wiser about the "madness of art" and the human costs that come with landscaping a fictional territory. For better or worse, Nathan's congenial turf turns out to be the Jews. Unfortunately, what he discovers – after publishing a scandalously successful exposé entitled *Carnovsky* – is that no analogues to his modernist precursors will wash. Try as he might, the mantle of exile that slipped so easily, so convincingly, around James Joyce's shoulders will not quite fit. Granted, there are no end of attacks, no end of those who would add Zuckerman to the list of Hamen and Hitler – names that deserve being blotted out – but the Zuckerman of *Zuckerman Unbound* (1981) craves approval rather than martyrdom. Down deep, he really can't believe that his antagonists are as angry as they claim, or that they would stay mad if he just had a chance to explain himself:

. . . not everybody was delighted by this book that was making Zuckerman a fortune. Plenty of people had already written to tell him off. "For depicting Jews in a peep-show atmosphere of total perversion, for depicting Jews in acts of adultery, exhibitionism, masturbation, sodomy, fetishism, and whoremongery," somebody with letterhead stationery as impressive as the President's had even suggested that he "ought to be shot." And in the spring of 1969 this was no longer just an expression. . . . Oh, Madam, if only you knew the real me! Don't shoot! I am a serious writer as well as one of the boys!

Zuckerman goes on to argue that his readers "had mistaken impersonation for confession," but mostly he protests too much – about the assorted difficulties that come with being rich-and-famous, about his misunderstood highmindedness, about his essential goodness, and perhaps most of all about his bad luck. After all, other writers – the modernist giants, for example – had it easier: "What would Joseph Conrad do? Leo Tolstoy? Anton Chekhov? When first starting out as a young writer in college he was always putting things to himself that way. . . ." The rub, of course, is that none of these writers grew up Jewish in Newark, had a Jewish mother pestered by reporters in Miami (*"I am very proud of my son and that's all I have to say. Thank you so much and goodbye."*), and had a dying father who kept faith with the conviction that "Tzena, Taena" is going to "win more hearts to the Jewish cause than anything before in the history of the world."

To be sure, there is much about Zuckerman's *tsoris* that has a familiar ring – not only in terms of Roth's canon (those who tsk-tsk about his candor; the shaky marriage sacrificed to the House of Fiction; grotesques such as Alvin Pepler, the Jewish Marine who won a bundle on a quiz show, only to be betrayed and then disgraced), but also in terms of the longer tradition of Jewish-American letters. Zuckerman is guilt-ridden about the money that crashes in as copies of *Carnovsky* roll off the presses. Sidewalk superintendents shower him with free advice: "You should buy a helicopter. That's how I'd do it. Rent the landing rights up on apartment buildings and fly straight over the dog-poop." After all, true is true: "Gone were the days when Zuckerman had only to worry about making money"; henceforth he would have to "worry about his money making money." In Abraham Cahan's scathing portrait of the Alrightnik – *The Rise of David Levinsky* (1917) – success is synonymous with an ashy taste. Some sixty years later Roth gives the garment district scenario a literary twist; now High Art, rather than the Spring line, can make one wealthy and estranged.

Zuckerman Unbound is, by all consensus, the weakest link in the chain of books that stretches from *My Life as a Man* to *The Facts*. No doubt part of the reason is that it is also the most conventional in terms of narrative structure. Alvin Pepler, the wacky know-it-all who can match Zuckerman paranoia for paranoia, self-righteousness for self-righteousness, even manages to get in a few good licks about Zuckerman's fictional treatment of autobiographical events:

> Fiction is not autobiography [Pepler's unfinished review of *Carnovsky* contends], yet all fiction, I am convinced, is in some sense rooted in autobiography, although the connection to actual events may be tenuous indeed, even nonexistent. . . . yet there are dangers in writing so closely to the heels of one's own immediate experience: a lack of toughness, perhaps; a tendency to indulgence; an urge to justify the author's ways to men.

One might suggest the same things about *Zuckerman Unbound*, adding a few grace notes about the ways in which self-laceration has been altered since the days when schlemiels shrugged their shoulders when they spilled the soup. But Pepler's point, however savvy, lacks sufficient context, enough sheer *force*, to be the counterweight that *Zuckerman Unbound* badly needs.

By contrast, *The Anatomy Lesson* (1983) gives Zuckerman's temper tantrums the postmodernist spin they deserve. "When he is sick," the novel's opening line declares, "every man wants his mother; if she's not around, other women must do." Zuckerman — ever the overachiever, the man of excess — is currently "making do" with four. More than two hundred pages later, Zuckerman, broken-down, hospitalized, and in the grip of sicknesses both mental and physical, will write on a clean notebook page: "WHEN HE IS SICK EVERY MAN NEEDS A MOTHER." But interior echoes are not the only reflexive touches that Roth introduces into this saga of Zuckerman's dark night of the soul. For example, once upon a time, Judge Wapter handed down Ten Indicting Questions from his chambers in Newark; now Zuckerman faces the seemingly innocent queries concocted by the editors of a school newspaper:

> The editors wanted to interview him about the future of his kind of fiction in the post-modernist era of John Barth and Thomas Pynchon. . . . would he please answer, at whatever length he chose, the ten questions on the sheet attached. . . . 1. *Why do you continue to write?* 2. *What purpose does your work serve?* 3. *Do you feel yourself part of a rearguard action in the service of a declining tradition?* 4. *Has your sense of vocation altered significantly because of the events of the last decade?*

For a Stephen Dedalus, griefs come in triads – family, church, and state. But since Stephen also fancies himself as a "priest of the eternal imagination," so do solutions: silence, exile, and cunning. In both cases, however, the world is neatly divided into trinities that remind us of his Irish Catholic upbringing and its abiding presence. By contrast, Zuckerman is plagued by Decalogues – and by their characteristic formulas of "Thou shalt not . . ." – without quite knowing how to respond in kind. Roth's agitated protagonists can, of course, call upon the Great Modernist Tradition, upon ghost writers from Henry James to Franz Kafka, but something vital is lost in the translation. *Their* world is, finally, not James's (one feels confident that *he* never had to eat his childhood dinners at the end of a knifeblade), nor is it Kafka's, despite the odd metamorphosis that turns Professor Kepish into a breast. Those smart enough to catch Roth's allusions are also smart enough to know a pale copy when they see one; and those more au courant with Judaica than Roth would have no hesitation using the word *l'havdal* (separation) to describe the phenomenon.

Nonetheless, Zuckerman continues to see himself as a beleaguered soul, rather like the corpse being dissected in Rembrandt's painting "The Anatomy Lesson." In Zuckerman's case, however, the fellow wielding the sharpest knife is Milton Appel, the moral critic who savaged him in an issue of *Inquiry*. Once again, those in the know knew that Roth had been tonguing a sore tooth ever since

Irving Howe published an article entitled "Reconsidering Philip Roth" in a 1973 issue of *Commentary*. Granted, Roth had folded criticism-as-counterweight into earlier novels, but this was bashing of a decidedly higher order. *This* attack, as Zuckerman puts it bitterly, "made Macduff's assault upon Macbeth look almost lackadaisical."

> . . . the Jews represented in *Higher Education* had been twisted out of human recognition by a willful vulgar imagination largely indifferent to social accuracy and the tenets of realistic fiction. Except for a single readable story, that first collection was tendentious junk, the by-product of a pervasive and unfocused hostility. The three books that followed had nothing to redeem them at all – mean, joyless, patronizing little novels, contemptuously dismissive of the complex depths. No Jews like Zuckerman's had ever existed other than as caricature, as literature that could interest grown people. None of the books could be said to exist at all, but were contrived as a species of sub-literature for the newly "liberated" middle-class, for an "audience," as distinguished from serious readers. Zuckerman was certainly no friend of Jews: *Carnovsky*'s ugly animus proved that.

Appel, in short, is no lightweight, and rail though Zuckerman might, his accusations sting. Even Appel's parentheticals – from a piece of private correspondence – find their way into Zuckerman's craw: "(and yes, I know that there's a difference between characters and authors; but I also know that grown-ups should not pretend that it's quite the difference they tell their students it is.)"

Wounded, weakened, sick nearly unto death, what is Zuckerman to do? Not since Bloom plumbed the depths of Nighttown (in Joyce's *Ulysses*) have there been such unrelenting abasement and such comic schlemielhood. He can, of course, rant-and-rail; he can name-call (e.g., Appel as the "Charles Atlas of Goodness"); he can amuse himself with parlor games that satirize Appel's titles and his methodology ("The Irrefutable Rethinkings of Milton Appel"; "Right and Rigid in Every Decade: The Polemical Spasms of a Hanging Judge"). But best of all, he can *become* Appel by transmogrifying him, *deconstructing* him, if you will, into a Milton Appel of a very different color – namely, the Al Goldstein look-alike who publishes a sleazy pornographic magazine called *Lickedy Split*. The result is a radical impersonation, one fixed no longer on the comic exaggerations and liberations by which Roth unleashes his Zuckerman, but rather on the grotesque playfulness that turns Appel into his Other.

Nor is this the only "victory" in a novel out to shore up fragments against Zuckerman's ruin. If he had played with the prospect of marrying Anne Frank in *The Ghost Writer*, in *The Anatomy Lesson* he toys with the idea of chucking fiction-writing altogether and becoming a doctor. No more subjectivity, no more inner life, no more burrowing back, no more "chewing on everything, seeking connections" – nobody criticizes the baby an obstetrician delivers; everyone welcomes the relief from pain that an anesthesiologist promises. *This* – rather than art – is the life that Zuckerman in middle-age hankers for. Besides, what better way to appease one's parents, to give them the ultimate *nachas* (joy), than by becoming, at long last, their son, the Jewish doctor?

Granted, this counterlife is not destined to succeed, as the novel's circular first sentence suggests, and as Zuckerman/Roth's continuing output makes all too clear. Indeed, what we have in *The Counterlife* (1987) is a version of Lonoff's aesthetic, but this time one that turns whole lives, rather than individual sentences, around. The result is akin to a kaleidoscope: characters become bits of colored glass that shift positions and perspectives (dead in one chapter, they spring back to life in the next) as Roth rotates his fictional cylinder in 180-degree twists. For Roth, "counter" has become an abiding, multipurpose prefix, the flashy way he slips the jabs of his opponents, and then justifies the *flash*. The cumulative effect of all this postmodernist carbonation, however, can exasperate those readers who prefer their fictions straight. As Cynthia Ozick points out in her recent collection of essays, *Metaphor & Memory* (1989):

The characters in Philip Roth's *The Counterlife* are so wilily infiltrated by Postmodernist inconstancy that they keep revising their speeches and their fates: you can't trust them even to stay dead. It goes without saying that we are forbidden to speculate whether the writer who imagined them is as anxiously protean, as cleft by doubt, as they.

But, of course, Ozick has her hunches, and given the sheer number of anxious speeches in *The Counterlife* about the imagination's deconstructive powers, why shouldn't she? It is, after all, not Zuckerman alone who talks compulsively about countertexts, who insists that "we are all the invention of each other, everybody a conjuration conjuring up everyone else," but Roth himself who marches to a similar drum in *The Facts*. As the postmodernist version of schlemielhood would have it, we are not only the architects of our own troubles but also the architects of other people's comically troubled stories. Rehearsing, yet again, the "facts" that had duped him into a marriage he fictionally chronicled in *My Life as a Man*, Roth talks about his life as if it were a slab of narratology:

> I was telling her who I thought I was and what I believe had formed me, but I was also engaged by a compelling form of narrative responsory. I was a countervoice, an antitheme, providing a naive challenge to the lurid view of human nature that emerged from her tales of victimized innocence.

Unfortunately, the Roth who sets out to introduce *The Facts* worries about presenting himself "in prose like this, undisguised." Until now he had always "used the past as the basis for transformation, for, among other things, a kind of intricate explanation to myself of my world" – and until now, the marvelous, transformed voice that resulted had largely belonged to Nathan Zuckerman. The question, then, is a simple but crucially important one – namely, "Is the book any good?" Only a Roth would think to ask it of a protagonist. And only Roth would append some thirty pages of Zuckerman's detailed, hard-hitting criticism to the bulk of "Roth's" autobiography.

Not surprisingly, Zuckerman is as unimpressed as he is discouraging. As he points out, the difference between the fictional character (namely, himself) who has obsessed Roth for the last decade and the autobiographical Philip Roth who takes such pains to tell us about his loving mother, his understanding father, and most of all his life as a nice Jewish son is precisely the difference between the dazzling excitements – and the deeper truths – of fiction and the flatter prose that results when Roth sticks too closely to the "facts":

> As for characterization, you, Roth, are the least completely rendered of all your protagonists. Your gift is not to personalize your experience but to personify it, embody it in the representation of a person who is *not* yourself. You are not an autobiographer, you're a personificator.

Indeed, Zuckerman makes a compelling case that *The Facts* is so "steeped in the nice-guy side" that it lacks struggle, lacks hubris, lacks madness – in short, that it comes up short in every category that gives Roth's fiction a distinctive thumbprint. "With this book," Zuckerman argues, "you've tied your hands behind your back and tried to write it with your toes."

Granted, Zuckerman is hardly a disinterested observer. Should Roth continue to pound away at the keyboard about the "real" exploits of Philip Roth rather than about the imagined, highly exaggerated ones of Nathan Zuckerman, where would *that* put the protagonist of the Zuckerman chronicles? Theirs has become a symbiotic relationship, a case of secret sharing so deep, so abiding, that even the word "need" hardly defines its character. As Zuckerman puts it:

> . . . I'd say you're still as much in need of me as I of you – and that I need you is indisputable. For me to speak of "my" anything would be ridiculous, however much there has been established in me the illusions of an independent existence. I owe everything to you, while you, however, owe me nothing less than the freedom to write freely. I am your permission, your indiscretion, the key to disclosure.

In short, *The Facts* seems to be cut from the same counter-cloth that patterned his earlier books, but with an important difference. This time Roth is out to justify his life (perhaps even to save it) by dropping the pretenses of fiction altogether. At long last, the persona behind the mask stands up, pushes the typewriter away, and tells his own story, in his own words, and with his own voice:

> Like you, Zuckerman, who are reborn in *The Counterlife* through your English wife, like your brother, Henry, who seeks rebirth in Israel with his West Bank fundamentalists, just as both of you in the same book miraculously manage to be revived from death, I too was ripe for another chance. If while writing I couldn't see exactly what I was up to, I do now: this manuscript embodies my counterlife, the antidote and answer to all those fictions that culminated in the fiction of you.

Apparently, a life crisis, if not a breakdown of considerable proportion, looms behind the autobiographical effort to smash through Roth's exhaustion with "masks, disguises, distortions, and lies." But those of us who have followed the long trail of tears, special pleading, and tantrums know enough to be on our guard. What is one to make, for example, of Roth's claim that he did *not* write *The Facts* to prove, once and for all, that "there is a significant gap between the autobiographical writer that I am thought to be and the autobiographical writer that I am"? As Maria Freshfield Zuckerman points out, there is a Latin term for such assertions – *occupatio*:

> It's one of those Latin rhetorical figures. "Let us not speak of the wealth of the Roman Empire. Let us not speak of the majesty of the invading troops, et cetera," and by not speaking about it you're speaking about it. A rhetorical device whereby you mention something by saying you're not going to mention it.

Nathan, not surprisingly, talks about autobiography in terms of its inevitable "countertext" – that is, the material the conscious, manipulative self edits out:

> You talk about what you were up against, what you wanted, what was happening to you, but you rarely say what you were like. You can't or won't talk about yourself as yourself, other than in this decorus way. . . . But obviously it's just as im-

possible to be proper and modest and well behaved and be a revealing autobiographer as it is to be all that and a good novelist. . . . this isn't unusual, really. With autobiography there's always another text, a countertext, if you will, to the one presented.

One could, of course, say much the same thing about Roth's fictions, where the alternating rhythms of construction and deconstruction, of text and countertext, of satiric attack and abject confession have been going on for some time, and where a nice Jewish boy's preoccupation with running wild gives every indication of continuing.

Saul Bellow and
the Special Comedy
of Urban Life

The big winter – gray Chicago scene –
ashen, with black strokes. In winter it
takes on a kind of mineral character.
After so many years I can still not
believe that the cause of this is entirely
natural but always suspect the presence
of a grim power whose materials are
streets, bungalows, tenements, naked
ironwork, grit, wind – an enchanter
whose idea is that everyone should take
the city to be a comedian, absurdist,
ironist, and relishes Chicago's
"realism"; he disguises his darkest
fantasies in its materiality, in
building, paving, drainage,
engineering, banking, electronics.
from Saul Bellow's
To Jerusalem and Back

To describe the inextricable connections between idea and naturalistic landscape, between the junk of randomness and an itch for some transcendental design, is, in effect, to explore the city. The very term has become a convenient shorthand of that place where competing interests and sheer numbers crunch uneasily together, where mental designs are expressed in their boldest relief. Saul Bellow has been our most articulate geographer of the urban condition, charting its assets and liabilities against the cunning that is history and those continuing needs that comprise the human spirit. More than any other American novelist, he knows what life in the city is really like:

> Cops have their own way of ringing a doorbell. They ring like brutes. Of course, we are entering an entirely new stage in the history of human consciousness. Policemen take psychology courses and have some feeling for the comedy of urban life. . . . Even the cops have seen *The Godfather*, *The French Connection*, *The Valachi Papers*, and other blast-and-bang thrillers. I was drawn to this gang stuff myself, as a Chicagoan, and I said, "I don't know anything." I dummied up, and I believe the police approved of this.

Bellow's protagonists may be attracted to realism, to those with solid credentials in "low-life expertise," but they cannot quite give themselves over to the brutal terms of such instruction. As Bellow once remarked in a lecture on Joyce's *Ulysses*: "Art makes one peculiarly observant, and the artist is often like one condemned to observe. The facts, presenting themselves, cannot be rejected. One is obliged to note them and to note them in a certain style." However, the facts of the quotidian matter are not the whole story. In Bellow's case, noting these facts "in a certain style" has resulted in fictions that are at once savvy, street-wise, thoroughly Chicagoan, and yet packing enough transcendental energy to leave plenty of room to speculate about higher powers and the individual soul.

By focusing upon the special comedy of urban life, I hope to suggest the ways in which Bellow's canon reduplicates Mark Schorer's formulation of "technique as discovery." As Joseph, the testy, hypercritical protagonist of *Dangling Man* (1944), would have it: "We are all drawn toward the same craters of the spirit – to know what we are and what we are for, to know our purpose, to seek grace." The protagonists of Bellow's later novels would, no doubt, agree, although they would probably express the sentiment with more flash, more stylistic punch, and almost certainly at extended length. In Joseph's case, however, the claustrophobic atmosphere of *Dangling Man* tethers him to his "journal" rather than the city per se. In effect, urban life becomes an occasion for quasi-philosophical speculations rather than an encounter with its gritty, naturalistic surfaces and bared knuckles. Joseph tends to gaze out windows rather than to walk down streets; nonetheless, his thickly textured reportage tells us a good deal about what cityscapes are and, more important, what they imply about modern life:

> The sun had been covered up; snow was beginning to fall. It had sprinkled over the black pores of the gravel and was lying in thin slips on the slanting roofs. I could see a long way from this third-floor height. Not far off there were chimneys, their smoke a lighter gray than the gray of the sky; and, straight before me, ranges of poor dwellings, warehouses, culverts, electric signs blankly burning, parked cars and moving cars, and the occasional bare plan of a tree. These I surveyed, pressing my forehead on the glass. It was my painful obligation to look and to submit to myself the invariable question: Where was there a particle of what, elsewhere, or in the past, had spoken in man's favor. . . . In all principle ways the human spirit must have been the same. Good apparently left fewer traces. And we are coming to know that we had misjudged whole epochs. Besides, the giants of the last century had their Liverpools and Londons, their Lilles and Hamburgs to contend against, as we have our Chicagos and Detroits.

As a self-declared "moral casualty of the war," Joseph broods about freedom and responsibility, alienation and community, introspective energies and existential angst, providing an index of difference between older, rough-and-ready exteriors (those Hemingwayesque postures Joseph regards as a mindless, insensitive brand of "hardboiled-dom") and Bellow's subtly rendered geography of the inner life. But that much said, let me hasten to add an important qualification: with the possible exception of those "alternatives" suggested by the alter-ego Joseph and addressed as *Tu As Raison Aussi*, contrary points of view are systematically excluded from both the record of Joseph's "inward transactions" and his ongoing search for big truths. The result is a novel that grows increasingly self-absorbed, its circles constricting inward as Joseph is thrown against the resources of an ever-shakier self.

With *The Adventures of Augie March* (1953), Bellow tests out Joseph's vague sense that "there is an element of the comic or fantastic in everyone" but without the feeling that one must keep a daily record of its ebbs and flows. Rather, Augie endlessly experiences what chance offers up, at the same time reserving the right to cut his losses if the propositions do not square with a "good enough fate." All this makes Augie a welcome relief from those of Bellow's protagonists who threaten to turn temporary setbacks into a permanent condition. At the same time, however, Augie is less a character in his own right than an embodiment of Whitmanian energy, a glob of Silly Putty bouncing off whatever obstacles loom around the next corner. Presumably Augie's faith in the "axial lines of life" will keep him headed in the right direction – and if there are detours, one can relax, learn to enjoy them. What Augie discovers, of course, is that an appetite for unbounded experience is nearly as hard to satisfy as his loftier sentiments about universal harmonies. Moreover, what Augie actually learns from all his frenetic, zigzagging motion is problematic at best. When Einhorn takes him to a brothel (as a combination graduation present and sexual rite de passage), Augie chalks up the resulting disappointment to the urban way things are:

> I knew it was basically only a transaction. But that didn't matter so much. Nor did the bed; nor did the room; nor the thought that the woman would have been amused – with as much amusement as could make headway against other considerations – at Einhorn and me, the great sensationist riding into the place on my back with bloodshot eyes and voracious in heart but looking perfectly calm and superior. Paying didn't matter. Nor using what other people used. That's what city life is.

In such matters Augie is the accommodationist par excellence. He saves his rebellious stands for those moments when well-meaning people attempt to finalize his "adoption." Chicago has more success teaching Augie's brother Simon all there is to know about the relationship between hard cash and cold-blooded power. He becomes the city incarnate, complete to his Palmer House haircut, tailored suit, and fancy car. But Augie is also living proof that clothes do not make the man. He slides through the tough spots on the force of his charm and his talent as a "good listener." Even Chicago cannot make a significant dent in his buoyant innocence. An immunity to "those Machiavellis of small street and neighborhood" comes with the picaresque territory. Augie may be fascinated by the power brokers and wheeler-dealers, but traveling along the "axial lines" presumably wards off any serious losses.

Such is not the case with Asa Leventhal and Tommy Wilhelm, those anxious believers in urban consensus who push or sink through their respective novels. Leventhal's victim/victimizer relationship with Allbee is framed by the irritation that results from being unsure about who runs either an individual subway train or the world in general. *The Victim* (1947) opens with Leventhal so preoccupied that he almost misses his stop; it ends with Allbee's claim that he has learned to accept his fate, that he is merely a "passenger" on life's train, "not the type that runs things." Leventhal, of course, cannot allow the provocative remark to go unchallenged: "Wait a minute, what's your idea of who runs things?" Unfortunately, the world does not wait any more than rush-hour subways do. The house lights dim, people are ushered to their seats, and the play begins.

Between Leventhal's first attempt to slow things down and his final, teleological question, New York City provides all the stimulation his irritability requires. By that I mean he has a genuine talent for turning vague uncertainties into principled suspicions, for converting floating anxieties into a vision of corporate blacklists. If Augie strenuously avoids specialization ("I don't know spot welding, I didn't know traffic management, I couldn't remove an appendix, or anything like that," he proudly declares), Leventhal is painfully aware of how specialized he has become. Even a city like New York can support relatively few trade journals. There will always be more qualified people than there are openings. True, Leventhal has a reasonably secure position at Burke-Beard and Company (although private industry generates more job anxieties than the civil-service post he resigned), but to be thankful for one's luck is also to realize how tenuous one's situation actually is. Allbee confirms Leventhal's equally stereotypical fear about Jewish persecution. Ironically enough, there is a certain amount of good cheer in discovering that you were right after all, that things are, indeed, as bad as you had imagined them to be.

In *Seize the Day* (1955), Tommy Wilhelm experiences something of the same catharsis by finally hitting rock bottom. His "day" is roughly divided between whining and desperation, between rationalizing past mistakes and plunging his last buck in the futures market. Dr. Adler – a retired diagnostician who diagnoses Tommy's problem as one of terminal "loserhood" – responds by washing his clinical hands of the whole business. For his "drowning" son, the best he can offer is a bit of free medical advice: ". . . there's nothing better than hydrotherapy when you come right down to it. Simple water has a calming effect." Tommy, on the other hand, stumbles to a different drummer; what about one's feelings, one's need for love, one's humanity?

Alas, New York operates on a different set of principles: nobody carries nobody! As Dr. Adler understands full well, there are times when you must cut your losses, pull the economic plug even if it means that the "waters of the earth . . . roll over" your own son. Cities are not places for the fainthearted, especially those who leap up when they behold that summer marks "the end of the lilacs."

At the same time, however, a place as filled with sharpers and con-artists as New York is not likely to let Tommy Wilhelm's pastoral itches go unscratched. For every schlemiel bent upon comic brands of self-destruction, there is a Tamkin ready to seize a $700 opportunity. If you play the stock market, Tamkin has a system; if you have an identity crisis, Tamkin has a psychoanalytic theory which throws in an extra soul free of charge.

Tommy divides his time between exercises in rationalization and flights of self-pity; there is little room for that ironic, inwardly directed laughter we associate with urban comedy. Even when Tommy sobs before the proxy coffin (surrounded by "official" mourners who wonder if he is "perhaps the cousin from New Orleans they were expecting," while others insist that no, "it must be somebody real close to carry on so"), he is more concerned about releasing pent-up tears than emulating Augie's notion of the *animal ridens*.

During the period between *Herzog* (1964) and *Humboldt's Gift* (1975), stage-center was monopolized by the protagonist-as-historian, rather than by the traditional concerns of the historical novel. As Bellow himself has suggested: "People don't realize how much they are in the grip of ideas. We live among ideas much more than we live in nature. . . . People's lives are already filled with mental design of one sort or another." In this regard, *Herzog*, *Mr. Sammler's Planet* (1970), and *Humboldt's Gift* form a loose trilogy, one concerned with the impress of ideas upon the fabric of contemporary culture and with the comic interaction between a culture's ideas and Bellow's embattled spokesmen. Unlike Tommy, these are protagonists more likely to utter ironic, urban prayers (*"Lead me not into Penn Station,"* quips Moses Herzog) than to flood the world in tears, more prone to trade wisecracks on the street than to hide between the pages of a solipsistic journal. In an age that pays both lip service and hard cash to the special importance of intellect, such protagonists grow to expect the gingerly treatment due an endangered species. There was a time in American literature when one was marked for special handling on other grounds. George Willard, for example, is filled with that sensitive stupidity which earmarks him as a good listener in *Winesburg, Ohio* and will, presumably, stand him in good stead in the big city. By contrast, Moses Herzog earns his way from grant to grant as a bonafide egghead – no small task, given a literary tradition that prefers to outshoot its antagonists and to restrict its reading to the labels on whiskey bottles.

Granted, life as the Academy's darling is a decidedly mixed blessing. People respond to Herzog with nearly equal doses of admiration and thinly veiled condescension. As the unwashed would have it, old saws like "If you're smart, why ain't you rich?" become the unspoken: "And if you were *really* so smart, how come you got cuckolded, fella?" This is bad enough, but those who appoint themselves as Herzog's instructors into the nature of the real are even worse. They elbow their way into his life with teeth bared and a stomach for the worst brutalities quotidian life can offer.

Herzog is peculiarly unequipped to deal with the hard edges of a reality seemingly cut off from time and wrenched from better, more humanistic continuities. What we need, he half-playfully insists, is a "good five-cent synthesis," one which would provide

> . . . a new angle on the modern condition, showing how life could be lived by renewing universal connections; overturning the last of the Romantic errors about the uniqueness of the Self; revising the old Western, Faustian ideology; investigating the social meaning of Nothingness.

It is a grand, wonderfully nutty dream, the stuff that makes protagonists such as Artur Sammler, Charlie Citrine, and the Benn Crader of *More Die of Heartbreak* (1987) tick. Bellow's urban comedians are more likely to be men of moral vision than accountants of hard fact. Their respective sagas are chapters in what Citrine calls "the Intellectual Comedy of the modern mind." In Herzog's case, everything militates against him making good on his early promise as a scholar: the sleazy cultural moment, Reality Instructors, Potato Lovers, nearly *any* woman, and, of course, Herzog himself. As the novel's opening line declares: "If I am out of my mind, it's all right with me thought Moses Herzog." His is a Blakean faith in the powers of raw persistence, in the excess which alone can lead to clear vision. But Herzog is as self-mocking as he is outwardly testy. For Bellow, the comic ironies that result are a way of knocking off some of the book's hard biographical edges, of keeping Herzog's meditative zeal in a tenuous equipoise with the shards of his local situation. It is also the stuff of which "suffering jokers" are made.

Herzog's "mental letters" are the best indication of this condition and of the stylistic advances Bellow had made since the days when protagonists were either confined within their adult brooding or condemned to a protracted adolescence. Herzog's letters allow for a mobility unmatched even by Augie's boast that he is "going everywhere! Why I am a sort of Columbus of those near-at-hand." Granted, Moses is more "mental traveller" than energetic picaro, but polemics serve roughly the same function for him that eagle hunting did for Augie. His ongoing "correspondence" argues with the living as well as the significant dead, in an attempt to clarify a world gone haywire. If, as Bellow once suggested, *Ulysses* is a "comedy of information," a novel in which popular science, snatches of song, folk wisdom, advertisement jingles, and the residue of cultural lore swirl through the confused but lovable Leopold Bloom, *Herzog* is a novel in which a larger, infinitely more sophisticated body of information presses upon Moses Herzog's exhausted brain. Very often these letters constitute an unspoken "No! in thunder" to the glib rhetoric of "crisis, alienation, apocalypse and destruction," to formerly rich ideas that have now become so commonplace that even middle-brows tout the void "as if it were so much salable real estate." But they also comment ironically on the Moses Herzog who admits that he "had been a bad husband – twice."

By deliberately breaking into the rhythm of his headiest thoughts, Herzog creates those nervous, zigzagging rhythms we associate with urban comedy. For example, after thoughtfully considering a passage from Kierkegaard's *Sickness Unto Death* ("dying the death means to experience death"), the comedian in Herzog cannot resist quipping, "Fine reading for a depressive!" In short, Herzog's capacity for analysis has a nasty habit of turning inward, of plying the tools of his historical trade on himself. After trying on a pair of Italian pants and a blazer with slender lapels and red-and-white stripes, Herzog notices that clothing stores hold up a triple mirror to nature, that history teaches us sobering lessons when our backs are turned; he responds by sticking out his tongue.

Herzog is crowded with such moments. One laughs without ever quite forgetting either Herzog's pain or the deadly earnestness of his quarrel with the Wastelanders. But that is because Bellow insists that if he were "obliged to choose between complaint and comedy, I would choose comedy, as more energetic, wiser and manlier." Since the mid-1970s, however, Bellow's natural gifts for comedy have taken something of a backseat to his penchant for preachiness – this, despite his insistence (in *More Die of Heartbreak*) that "one has to feel sorry for people in . . . an explanatory bind. Or else (a better alternative) one can develop an eye for the comical side of this." *To Jerusalem and Back* (1976), for example, presented us with a nonfictional Saul Bellow who turned out to be as perplexed about the Middle East as anybody else; and his *Nobel Lecture* (1976) proved that, once behind the lectern, Bellow could also be as long-winded, even as slightly pedantic, about world literature as an Oxford don. In short, one began to miss the short leash on which Bellow had kept most of his brainy protagonists. After all, the richness of *Herzog*'s style is precisely that density which allows comedy, pain, wisdom, and seriousness something approaching equal space. The following passage represents the phenomenon in ways that none of his subsequent fiction can match:

> *Survival!* he noted. *Till we figure out what's what. Till the chance comes to exert a positive influence.* (Personal responsibility for history, a trait of Western culture, rooted in the Testaments, Old and New, the idea of the continual improvement of human life on this earth. What else explained Herzog's ridiculous intensity?) *Lord, I ran to fight in Thy holy cause, but kept tripping, never reached the scene of the struggle.*

Mr. Sammler's Planet, for example, begins at a point well beyond Herzog's rage for a synthesizing book or even the exhaustion that stretches Herzog across his pastoral hammock. Artur Sammler casts his "one good eye" on the junk of contemporary culture from a vantage point beyond sensuality. In this sense Sammler is less an extension of the romantic Herzog than he is a variation of the themes of Yeats's "Sailing to Byzantium." Caught in a city which has added genital-bullying to our century's "mackerel-crowded" landscape, he also concludes that "that is no country for old men." It is also not the time or the place for further "explanations":

> You had to be a crank to insist on being right. Being right was largely a matter of explanations. Intellectual man had become an explaining creature. Fathers to children, wives to husbands, lecturers to listeners, experts to laymen, colleagues to colleagues, doctors to patients, man to his own soul, explained.

Nonetheless, *Mr. Sammler's Planet* is a book composed of exactly these sorts of "explanations." If the subways were hot and overcrowded in *The Victim*, things have worsened steadily since. Sammler walks cautiously through "invariably dog-fouled" streets, no longer surprised that the counterculture's young look "autochthonous" or that one must search like Diogenes for a functioning telephone booth.

In *Mr. Sammler's Planet* the rage for a "charmed and *interesting* life" turns minor characters into menagerie grotesques and the city itself into a theatre of decadence. That much about Bellow's fiction has remained constant – in *More Die of Heartbreak* (where Fishl Vilitzer, the local representative of a West Coast maharishi, cons potential investors into playing the market "from a spiritual base"); in those who surround Clara Velde, the protagonist of *A Theft* (1989); and most recently in the machinations that give rise to the Mnemosyne Institute in *The Bellarosa Connection* (1989). Sammler hectors nearly everyone as if he were an East European Gibbon and this was the decline-and-fall of New York.

Bellow's earlier fiction was careful to keep such rancor at least half hidden behind comic masks, but with Sammler, as well as those who follow in his increasingly neoconservative footsteps (e.g., Dean Albert Corde, Kenneth Trachtenberg, Teddy Regler, and the unnamed narrator of *The Bellarosa Connection*), enough sociopolitical *narishkeit* (foolishness) is apparently enough. Besides, Sammler enjoys his role as a self-styled Jeremiah among the unclean who care as little for authority as they do for Old World "culture." Not since the days of T. S. Eliot has there been such an eloquent, and extended, appeal on behalf of reestablishing that necessary relationship between tradition and the individual talent: "Antiquity accepted models, the Middle Ages – I don't want to turn into a history book before your eyes – but modern man, perhaps because of collectivization, has a fever of originality."

Mr. Sammler's Planet is, in effect, a three-tiered world: on the naturalistic level, sexuality asserts a chaotic power, one expressed in bold relief by the elegant, Black pickpocket; Lal (whose manuscript is an Eastern version of Norman Mailer's *Fire on the Moon*) projects an overhanging lunar metaphor; while Sammler himself directs our attention to those depths wherein each of us can rediscover the terms of our human contract. Ironically enough, of the three possibilities, it is the first that garners the largest amount of sheer space. *Mr. Sammler's Planet* is as filled with urban oddballs as it is with realistic detail. It is, in short, a world that begins to look more and more like Shula-Slawa's shopping bags – crammed to the bursting point with all manner of eccentric goods. The book's minor characters tend to irritate the priggish Sammler, but their lapsability is an index of his own strength. *He* can explain the mention designs that lie just behind the city's veneer of hustle and tough talk. In this effort he will be joined by Dean Albert Corde, a man out to expose Chicago's dark underside to the readers of *Harper's*. In Sammler's case, being a wise old man means that desperate people will seek out his sage advice; for Albert Corde, high-class journalism provides the outlet. With both protagonists, however, it is the city that calls forth their respective passions and their respective "lectures."

In similar ways *Humboldt's Gift* is at once a prolonged, often painful meditation on the responsibilities of the living to the dead and a comic paean to Chicago, full of zany romps through its streets and buildings. The result is God's plenty both of heady thought and urban savvy. The story of Charles Citrine is divided into two separate but unequal parts – backward glances at what he calls his "significant dead" and the forward motions of a life growing increasingly cluttered.

Von Humboldt Fleisher epitomizes the lyric poet extraordinaire. During the 1930s his *Harlequin Ballads* was "an immediate hit," the stuff of which literary fame – and literary power – is fashioned. But an appetite like Humboldt's depends upon calculated restlessness, a fight to the finish between life as it is and what his poetry might make it become. If Goethe had insisted, at the end, on "More light!" poor Humboldt required an even wider range of excesses: more enemies, more influence, more sex, more money, more. . . . As Citrine puts it, "Humboldt wanted to drape the world in radiance, but he didn't have enough material."

Humboldt haunts the novel both as an abiding presence and a fearful reminder. Had I. B. Singer written the novel, Humboldt would surely have been an invading *dybbuk*; Bellow seems willing to settle for the dead poet as one of Citrine's more troublesome ghosts of the heart. Humboldt had spent his life "pondering what to do between *then* and *now*, between birth and death to satisfy certain great questions," and now Citrine must face the awful possibility that the

costs of that quest had outstripped its accomplishments. For one
thing, the centers of power had shifted, reducing Humboldt to an
object America can love but need not take seriously, much less fear.

Humboldt is, of course, not the only casualty of America's unflinching toughness. Citrine's elegiac tone reveals as much about
himself as it does about his poetic master. Humboldt's epical list of
"sacred words" (e.g., Alienation, Waste Land, the Unconscious) is
a poignant reminder of those days when, as Lionel Abel once put it,
New York was a very Russian city, a "metropolis yearning to belong
to another country." Which is to say Von Humboldt Fleisher was the
American-Jewish renaissance in powerful miniature. By contrast,
Citrine had been "too haughty to bother with Marxism, Freudianism,
the avant-garde, or any of these things that Humboldt, as a culture
Jew, took so much stock in." Like Bellow himself, Citrine operates
on the gut feeling that if ten people believe in an idea, it could not
possibly have much value. Both author and character prefer the
naturalistic turf of Chicago (where one is forced, in Citrine's words,
to become "a connoisseur of the near-nothing") to the assorted
"isms" that New York intellectuals generate. And yet, Citrine finds
himself uncomfortably famous as the graph of his success rises in
direct proportion to Humboldt's decline.

Citrine bears more than a little resemblance to Moses Herzog.
He too has a grand book more in mind than on paper, and he too
suffers all the pangs of a life "in great disorder." But the Hum-
boldt/Citrine relationship is also a version of the psychological
sharing Bellow had explored in *The Victim.* Humboldt's accusations, however loony or unfounded or both, cannot be dismissed
out of hand. Citrine's meditations are filled with the suspicion that
Humboldt may have been right after all. Has the intellectually
competitive life turned him (however unintentionally, however un-
consciously) into an "operator," an enemy of true art?

Penance requires nothing less than an "inspired levitation" toward the truth, a project big enough to prevent the "leprosy of
souls." It is a tall order, as tiring as it is impossible. And, not surprisingly, carrying the weight of Western thought on his shoulders
takes a comic toll.

The result is a Charles Citrine ("Pulitzer Prize, Legion of Honor, father of Lish and Mary, husband of A, lover of B, a serious person, and a card") who tries to square the mystical pronouncements of Rudolph Steiner (*Knowledge of the Higher Worlds and Its Attainment*, 1923) with the concrete surfaces of Chicago. The effort is valiant (quixotic?) enough, but likely to end in what Citrine's analyst calls "melancholia . . . interrupted by fits of humor." Even the much harried Artur Sammler had more success reading his Meister Eckhart in peace. Citrine begins a Steinerian meditation, only to find himself interrupted by angry knocks from the outside. In Citrine's case, the knocks include those by Reality Instructors who hector him about his dreaminess; lovable con-artists with schemes for projected books or an African mine; racketeers who run the gamut from those who dress like gentlemen and play paddleball to those who batter expensive automobiles with baseball bats; quack spiritualists; sensuous women; and those ultimate heavies in Bellow's universe – lawyers representing an estranged wife. Citrine suffers them all – and himself – with comic grace. After all, he has long recognized that "in business Chicago, it was a true sign of love when people wanted to take you into money-making schemes." But there are other, more literary reasons as well. Characters like Citrine require a thickly textured counterbalancing if the novel is to avoid spinning off into those "higher worlds" Rudolph Steiner writes about. The city provides Bellow with a necessary comic grounding, a way of keeping Charles Citrine under pressure and in what he calls his "Chicago state":

> . . . I infinitely lack something, my heart swells, I feel a tearing eagerness. The sentient part of the soul wants to express itself. There are some of the symptoms of an overdose of caffeine. At the same time I have a sense of being the instrument of external powers. They are using me either as an example of human error or as the mere shadow of desirable things to come.

I suspect this comes as close to a description of Bellow's own creative processes as we are likely to get. In *More Die of Heartbreak*, Kenneth Trachtenberg, the narrative voice out to simultaneously protect and justify his dreamy, distracted uncle, puts it this way:

My work was cut out for me: I was to help my dear uncle to defend himself. I didn't suppose that the Layamons meant him great harm; only they weren't likely to respect his magics or to have the notion of preserving him for the sake of his gifts. There was quite a lot at stake here. I can't continually be spelling it out [although, unfortunately, Kenneth does precisely that in the novel]. As: the curse of human impoverishment as revealed to Admiral Byrd in Antarctica; the sleep of love in human beings as referred to by Larkin; the search for sexual excitements as the universal nostrum; the making of one's soul as the only project genuinely worthy of undertaking.

Trachtenberg's last phrase is especially important because, as we learn earlier in the novel, "The city is the expression of the human experience it embodies and this includes all personal history." The result is that if a Benn Crader, an Albert Corde, a Clara Velde, and the unnamed narrator of *The Bellarosa Connection* are to make their respective souls, the smithy on which they will be forged is the city.

All of which brings my discussion of Bellow's sense of urban comedy full circle, back to the epigraph about the city as "a grim power" behind material artifacts. As Humboldt would have it: ". . . there's something perverse with that guy [Citrine]. After making this dough, why does he bury himself in the sticks? What's he in Chicago for?" But that is exactly the point: Humboldt instructed Citrine in the good, the true, and the beautiful from beyond the grave; Cantabile provides lower-browed instruction on the streets. Citrine – and Bellow – need both kinds, and roughly the same yoking of disparate elements by comedy is true for other protagonists one meets as Bellow's canon continues its cranky love affair with urban life.

Revisionist Thought,
Academic Power,
and the Aging
American Intellectual

*If you venture to think in America, you
also feel an obligation to provide a
historical sketch to go with it, to
authenticate or legitimize your
thoughts. So it's one moment of
flashing insight and then a quarter of
an hour of pedantry and tiresome
elaboration – academic gabble.*
from Saul Bellow's
More Die of Heartbreak

A healthy skepticism about what often passes in America
for intellectualism is neither a new nor an unwelcome
phenomenon. Indeed, some of the liveliest and most unflinching critiques of the life of the mind have been
mounted by intellectuals themselves. They have worried, for example, about the fit of various mental designs with quotidian life;
ideas have been debated, tested, and haggled over by the very intellectuals for whom ideas are a way of life. Increasingly, however,
wholesale dismissals of intellectualism are gaining currency, and
intellectuals themselves no longer think in the broad, social terms
that once defined their mission.

If a noun is known by the adjectives it keeps company with,
then, at least in America, such nouns as "humorist," "politician,"
and – most of all – "intellectual" are known most often by the ad-

jective "mere." This is disheartening enough for the persons involved, but the plight of the intellectual is even worse; though few ever heard of a *so-called* politician or a *pseudo*-humorist, these adjectives are regularly applied to the noun "intellectual." Because Americans are so deeply suspicious of ideas and the power they carry, making sense of American intellectual life has never been easy. As a people, we are equally suspicious of history and the history of ideas, preferring enterprises credentialed by the heart rather than the mind. Just as important is the national preoccupation with a self-glorifying set of myths – a force that intellectual disinterestedness can seldom match. We have so long swooned to the language of national specialness, to visions of America as a charmed land where dreams of the "new and improved" must inevitably flourish, that we have lost the power to discriminate between national politics and toothpaste ads.

More than a hundred years ago, Henry James, reflecting on the cultural conditions that severely delimited even so great an imaginative writer as Nathaniel Hawthorne, imagined that the Civil War would forever sound an end to our nation's simple, uncritical faith that "there were no difficulties in the programme, no looming implications, no rocks ahead." What he envisioned was nothing less than the loss of our collective innocence and its replacement by what would be a decidedly new American type – a "more critical person than his complacent and confident grandfather." One need only cite the legacy of Ronald Reagan to suggest how wide of the mark James's prediction was. Americans love to hear about the "shining cittie on a hille" that was our first, and perhaps deepest, American Dream, but do not want to reflect upon the fierce intolerance for other creeds present in Puritan John Winthrop's words as he uttered them aboard the *Arbella*. Boosters rather than knockers carry the American day.

But while it is true that philistines are still among us (witness the recent flap in Congress about "pornographic art" and National Endowment for the Arts funding), the days are over when a Richard Hofstadter could describe anti-intellectualism as "a resentment and suspicion of the life of the mind and of those who are considered to represent it; and a disposition constantly to minimize the value of that life" and thereby conjure up images of the *Boobus americanus*. Now, those most wary of intellectuals sport horn-rimmed spectacles and three-piece suits, dine at trendy restaurants, and subscribe to magazines such as *National Review, New Criterion,* and *Commentary*. They equate being tough-minded with playing realpolitik's hardball and divide their time between rolling their eyeballs whenever they hear the L-word and bashing any intellectuals still so unfashionable as to be one inch left of center. Given the choice they, like William F. Buckley, would prefer to be governed by the first hundred names in the Cambridge telephone directory rather than by the Harvard faculty.

Paul Johnson, who served as staff writer and then as editor of London's left-wing the *New Statesman* from 1955 to 1970 before taking a sharp turn to the right, is a representative case of the new revisionism at work. His earlier books (e.g., *A History of the Jews* [1987] and *Modern Times: The World from the Twenties to the Eighties* [1985]) were distinguished by fair-minded scholarship and graceful writing. By contrast, his latest effort – *Intellectuals* (1988) – is a hastily researched, altogether mean-spirited affair, filled with the prudery and downright nastiness that often characterize neo-conservatism, British-style. At its center is nothing less than what Americans will recognize as the Watergate formula – what did you know, and when did you know it? – as applied to those who dragged their heels about Stalin or who refused to be more of an anticommunist than Johnson's right-thinking, conservative heroes.

For Johnson, the essential point about intellectuals is that they are not to be trusted – not now, not during the sad, bloody sweep of the twentieth century, and indeed not at any time since the French Revolution. Not only do intellectuals specialize in writing manifestos about how people should conduct themselves, but they are also ruthlessly single-minded in orchestrating the ways by which these prescriptions might be translated into action. It is, Johnson argues, "time to examine their record, both public and personal," and to allow this history to speak for itself:

> How did they run their own lives? With what degree of rectitude did they behave to family, friends and associates? Were

they just in their sexual and financial dealings? Did they tell, and write, the truth? And have their own systems stood up to the tests of time and praxis?

Not surprisingly, the "record" – from Rousseau, Shelley, and Marx to Russell, Sartre, and Baldwin – is not salutary. Taken as a group, Johnson's gallery of intellectual rogues is much more likely to care about humanity in general than about individual persons, to cheat on wives or mistresses and psychologically batter children, to cadge money from long-suffering friends and, in some cases, from underpaid employees, and most of all to be obsessed with self-aggrandizement and career building. In short, after reading Johnson one would not relish the prospect of spending a holiday weekend with such characters. Johnson brings us the debunking news about the books and authors our culture treats (or, perhaps more correctly, *used* to treat) with reverence as if the gap between great ideas and great persons were in fact news. That human nature – even in persons with good ideas – has its sleazy side is not news, certainly not in the 1990s. What makes Johnson's attack noteworthy is, first, the urbane wit that he brings to his relentless raids of biographies for undercutting detail and, second, the selective vision that directs his indignation entirely toward intellectual scoundrels on the Left. Conspicuous by their absence are Yeats, Pound, and Eliot, Nietzsche, Heidegger, and de Man.

We can see foreshadowings of Johnson's intellectual doubt in the special case of Henry Adams, a man who dabbled – sometimes impressively – in a wide range of disciplines (history, biography, anthropology, the natural sciences, medieval scholarship, painting, and sculpture), but always as a self-professed, and usually self-abnegating, amateur. His *The Education of Henry Adams* (1907) points toward the modernism that provided one pillar of support for a generation of intellectuals who came of age in the 1940s, but it did so in curious ways. For Adams meant to write an *anti*-autobiography, whose subject was, among other things, the impossibility of acquiring an adequate education in the modern world, either at Harvard or, indeed, anywhere else. Unlike the generations of his illustrious and aristocratic forebears, his lot was to live among uncertainties, deep-seated anxieties, and doubts. He may have taken his characteristic pose from the Enlightenment's conception of a man of letters, the philosophe in the mold of Voltaire and Diderot, yet everything about this oddly disappointed man points toward modernism.

Nothing about Adams himself – not his aristocratic background, not his wealth and snobbery, not his social connections and Harvard crimson – would have ingratiated him to the group that formed around *Partisan Review* and later came to be known as the New York intellectuals. They were a feisty plebeian bunch, out to impose (or perhaps superimpose) a European model of culture onto America's native ground. But on one essential matter they would have made common cause, and that is the definition of an intellectual as one who specializes in being a nonspecialist.

Nearly fifty years ago, Philip Rahv pointed out that American fiction was longer on what he called "the cult of experience" than it was on either intellectuals or ideas. As things turned out, however, Rahv did not have to wait long to have ideas make their way into American fiction, for in the very next year his own journal – *Partisan Review* – published a piece by a young fictionist named Saul Bellow. And what soon followed was the story of one distracted intellectual after another stump-speeching his way through Bellow's fiction. Bellow himself makes no apologies for those of his protagonists who grapple with high-minded ideas, but he is quick to count himself among the streetwise.

It is probably a measure of Bellow's greatness that nearly as much critical space is devoted to branding him an anti-intellectual as is devoted to bemoaning the thick texture of allusions that characterizes his style. Faulkner suffered a similar fate, albeit with a decidedly different twist: many of his Southern readers thought him entirely too liberal, while many in the North bitterly complained that he wasn't liberal enough. The point, of course, is that fiction writers are more likely to be interested in the thousands of small choices that bring a landscape to life and that reveal character far more tellingly than exposition ever can. Faulkner found his "postage stamp of native soil" in the Yoknapatawpha County he invented and reigned over as "sole owner and proprietor"; Bellow alternately frets and swoons in what one protagonist calls his "Chicago state."

Let me make Bellow's point in a slightly different way: ideas — naturally, necessarily — come with a fictional territory. In Faulkner's case, ideas are as much a part of the landscape as dogtrot cabins and magnolia trees; with Bellow, we feel their presence in skyscrapers and crowded subways. In short, the question to ask is not, "Does a novel contain ideas?" (indeed, how could the case be otherwise) but, rather, "How good are they?" And surprising though it may sound, the answer — first proposed by Diana Trilling in a review of Bellow's *The Victim* (1947) — is that good novelists have good ideas, and bad novelists bad ones. Granted, the distinction may strike certain of my theoretically inclined colleagues either as hopelessly simpleminded or as impossibly vague, but when faced with two novels that share much by way of subject matter and cultural context — say, Bellow's *Herzog* (1964) and Norman Mailer's *An American Dream* (1965) — Trilling's yardstick is a serviceable one indeed.

The same benchmarks that we apply to fictionists can, and should, be applied to those we usually group together as intellectuals. Indeed, with many of the intellectuals we rightly hold in high regard — one thinks of Edmund Wilson, George Orwell, or Mary McCarthy — their writings cover not only a wide range of cultural subjects but also a considerable gamut of creative genres. For Johnson, political postures alone separate heroes from villains, however much he muddies the water by ad hominem attacks. But what distinguishes these writers are their contributions to belles lettres, to the essay as a form of writing worthy unto itself, and to the essay as a mode of engagement with a culture's sense of itself — sometimes sharply polemical, sometimes given to utopian impulses; at one turn, responding to events, at another helping to supply the general atmosphere in which events happen.

That these writers stood tall in an age when the literary essay mattered, and when there was a giddy sense that important struggles were being waged on behalf of the politics of the Left and the art of the avant-garde, is now a matter of consensus. At the same time, however, merely to recite the names of those who joined them in the pages of *Partisan Review*, in *Politics*, in *Kenyon Review* and *Sewanee* during the 1940s and 1950s – Dwight Macdonald, Irving Howe, John Crowe Ransom, Robert Penn Warren, Harold Rosenberg, Daniel Bell, Lionel Trilling – is to realize how difficult it would be to come up with a similarly impressive list for the 1980s. Granted, some possible nominees spring to mind – a Susan Sontag here, a Michael Walzer there – but the plain truth is that those in the know know that the centers of power have shifted. No doubt Johnson would make a case for the revisionist thought one encounters in magazines such as Norman Podhoretz's *Commentary* or Hilton Kramer's *New Criterion*, but the excitements that once swirled around intellectual quarterlies now cluster around increasingly specialized academic journals and presses, each with its requisite rites of passage and distinctive jargon. Those unfamiliar with the dense textures of deconstruction and largely committed to Jacques Derrida's latest pronouncements need not apply to *Diacritics* – as either readers or writers; those whose acquaintance with Freud does not include a refresher course in Jacques Lacan will have great difficulty making their way through the spring list of publications by many of our most distinguished university presses.

That academic life should promote specialization is understandable enough. But academic life also creates its own version of the territorial imperative. Even a disinterested observer of, say, the annual meetings of the Modern Language Association (MLA) cannot miss the cultural lobbying that each year produces a thick "Program" issue of PMLA (Publication of the Modern Language Association) which lists literally hundreds of panels and special sessions and cash bars devoted to every possible shading along the special-interest spectrum. Those who play the game best know that one first invents a kingdom and then declares oneself its king. The result, depending on the perspective, is either an academic version of Jesse Jackson's rainbow coalition or a fair approximation of Babel. One thing, however, becomes clear as the more than 12,000 participants and three days of shop talk wind down – namely, very few of the individual sessions are conducted in anything that remotely resembles standard English, and this includes the obligatory programs held by those whose business is the teaching of freshman composition.

By the ordinary measures of the MLA, Socrates – though he fits many of Johnson's criteria for an intellectual (he had a troubled domestic life with Xantippe and, more important, hatched elaborate plans for the totalitarian governing of what he called "The Republic") – was no intellectual. After all, as Joseph Heller points out in one of *Picture This*'s more acerbic asides:

> [Socrates] was not anyone's idea of an intellectual.
> Other philosophers founded schools . . . Socrates had no school. . . .
> He had no fellow scholars, colleagues, or associates with whom he worked or formed a group, no movement, methodology, or ideology of which he was the center of inspiration. He was not ambitious. He did not even write for a magazine.

Closer to our time, poor Moses Herzog – scribbling away at one of his "mental letters" – remarks that "*The people who come to evening classes are only ostensibly after culture. Their great need, their hunger, is for good sense, clarity, truth – even an atom of it. People are dying – it is no metaphor – for lack of something real to carry home when day is done. See how willing they are to accept the wildest nonsense.*" Roughly the same things might now be said about academic conferences, but with this important caveat: those in the thick of the horse-swapping may have moments when they suspect that the emperor has no clothes, but they also know that elbowing one's way onto a panel or into the pages of a professional journal makes life mighty comfortable on an academic raft.

Two recent conferences might serve as illustrations of my case. To be sure, the agendas differed, and the respective fireworks they generated may have struck outsiders as so many popguns, but for sheer theatre and confrontational dynamics, they were academic versions of the "Morton Downey, Jr., Show." The first one was billed as "The Writer in the Jewish Community: An Israel–North American Dialogue" and took place in Berkeley, California, in October 1988. That there are conferences focusing on "Jewish writing" – complete with squabbling about its precise definition, estimates of its triumphs and shortcomings, and contradictory prophecies regarding its future – has long been a fact of the academic landscape, but the Berkeley conference differed in two important respects: the sheer stature of its participants and the pervasive sense that Jewish writing had taken a sobering, perhaps irreversible turn.

Let me address the former – and easier – matter first. This was a conference with very deep pockets thanks to its funding by the National Foundation for Jewish Culture, Keshet-Cultural Projects Promotion, Ltd. (Israel), and the CRB Foundation of Canada. Whatever else may be said of Jewish life – in America, in Canada, in Israel – organizations committed to cultural programming in general, and to dialogue in particular, continue to thrive. At every possible occasion the audience was reminded about those picking up the tab and aiming their videotape machines, and no speakers – be they Israeli or American – could escape the banner of the National Foundation for Jewish Culture draped conspicuously over the lectern.

Academics, of course, are a skeptical bunch, not at all shy about biting the hands that served up such intellectual treats as Cynthia Ozick and Irving Howe, Stanley Kunitz and Amos Oz, Max Apple and High Nissenson (to name but a handful of the literary celebrities in attendance) – all at a single conference and crowded into a single auditorium. Several hundred people attended, not because they had an allegiance to Jewish organizations or even because they believed that the difficult issues separating Israeli writers from their Jewish-American counterparts would be settled, but rather because they would have an opportunity to watch individuals with first-rate minds grapple with tough questions and occasionally to lock horns with each other.

As it turned out, those who hankered for redder meat did not have to wait long. Ruth Wisse (author of *The Schlemiel as Modern Hero* [1971] and *A Little Love in Big Manhattan* [1988] and a frequent contributor to *Commentary*) took those Israeli writers on the Left to task for not being militant enough – that is, neoconservative enough – in their treatment of Arabs and the West Bank question, and she earned a stinging rebuke from Irving Howe for her pains; Michael Lerner, editor of *Tikkun*, a magazine solidly positioned on what can only be called the neo-religious Left, flooded the hall with brochures touting *Tikkun* and did what he could from the floor (he was not numbered among the official participants) to keep political tensions at a brisk boil; Amos Oz, the Israeli author, was as charming and as personable as one could be when bearing the bad news that American Jewry represents "a museum culture"; and Anton Shammas, probably the most anomalous figure in this very mixed deck (he is the Israeli Arab whose Hebrew novel, *Arabesques*, was both a best-seller and a troubling sensation), peered over the banner so thoughtfully provided by the National Foundation for Jewish Culture and told the audience: "I am Rambo, your worst nightmare."

What I found troubling was not the caucusing in the hallways or even the sharp words orchestrated for the videocameras, but rather the heady talk about what the imagination could or could not do – as if this were a matter that critics and scholars and conferences could decide. At one point Kafka was dragged into the discussion as yet another example of what the "culture of Europe" once had made possible, and what the Holocaust had forever destroyed, as if anything – with the possible exception of Kafka's father – could explain the eerie fascination of Kafka's stories.

By contrast, the James Joyce birthday bash-cum-symposium held at the University of Miami (February 2–4, 1989) restricted its focus to a single issue – namely, the Hans Gabler edition of *Ulysses*, published with great fanfare in 1986 and the subject of a controversy that has raged in the pages of the *New York Review of Books* since John Kidd called the edition to task in a scathing article entitled "The Scandal of 'Ulysses'" (June 30, 1988).

Normally, a conference devoting itself to the minutiae of scholarly editing would not attract a large crowd, but then again, Gabler's edition was hardly an ordinary text. To those who packed the auditorium, *Ulysses* is less a novel than *the* modernist bible. And since the University of Miami had enough contacts and hard cash to assemble all the important international players – Hans Gabler from Germany, Philip Gaskel from England, Fritz Zenn from Switzerland, and of course John Kidd from the United States – this was a rare opportunity to watch a battle royal in the flesh rather than merely following it in print.

Here, as in Berkeley, life had a way of imitating art and ending as bad theatre. Central casting could not have come up with better choices than the impeccably dressed Hans Gabler, who played the role of the dapper Establishment scholar to perfection, or the rumply suited, wildly bearded John Kidd (his "evidence" against Gabler literally bursting the seams of his briefcase), who played the maverick scholar. Add a milieu in which every word uttered by participant and audience member alike was dutifully recorded and the result was an atmosphere in which only fools or those very confident about their Joycean credentials rushed to the nearest microphone.

That the editions of *Ulysses* prior to Gabler's were jampacked with errors is, of course, something that all Joyceans agree about, but after all the complicated reasons why this is so have been explored (e.g., the French typesetters who hadn't the foggiest idea of what they were setting; Joyce's predilection – as a consummate "putter-inner" – to add ever more complexities, puns, correspondences, and parallels to his already complicated galleys; and not least of all, his failing eyesight), it is possible – just possible – that Joyce, being Joyce, intended that the faithful should break their heads over precisely the sort of conundrums that gave rise to Gabler's computer-assisted edition and then occasioned a conference in which several hundred scholars would seriously debate the question of whether it was, or was not, Holy Writ. One had the sinking feeling – as talk about editing principles, manuscript "reliability," and computer technology grew ever more complicated, and then as if to thicken the plot, when charges of conspiracy, profiteering, and plain bad faith were added to the mix – that most of the audience had forgotten that *Ulysses*, in whatever edition one happens to read it, remains what it has always been: a great comic novel.

Not surprisingly, the jury is still out on the merits or fatal flaws of Gabler's edition, but those who have long suspected that Joyce's quip about Shakespeare study as "the happy hunting ground of minds that have lost their balance" might more accurately be applied to Joyce scholarship had their suspicions confirmed. The same people, I should hasten to add, have their doubts about other academics, especially when these academics are less prone to humor in general, and to self-mocking humor in particular, than most Joyceans are.

The truth is that intellectual life, as it is conducted in our universities, has always been good for a wickedly satiric laugh; nonetheless, it would be hard to imagine a richer time for a novelist like David Lodge. *Small World* (1984), his comic account of literary theoreticians on the make, is perhaps the definitive *O tempora! O mores!* At one point in the novel, Morris Zapp (an American post-structuralist who knows a good scam when he sees one) bedazzles his British audience with a lecture/performance entitled "Criticism as Striptease":

> "To understand a message is to decode it. Language is a code. *But every decoding is another encoding.* . . . [But] this is not a striptease, it is all strip and no tease, it is the terpsichorean equivalent of the hermeneutic fallacy of recuperable meaning, which claims that if we remove the clothing of its rhetoric from a literary text we discover the bare facts it is trying to communicate. . . . To read is to surrender oneself to an endless displacement of curiosity and desire from one sentence to another. The text unveils itself before us, but never allows itself to be possessed; and instead of striving to possess it we should take pleasure in its teasing."

Confronted by such balderdash, the British — to their credit — write academic novels; by contrast, American academics vigorously lobby the dean so that they can establish a Chair of Post-Structuralist Study and perhaps entice Zapp to join their faculty.

The marked differences in attitude, in style, and most of all in essential vision between the intellectual and the academic bring to mind the antagonistic forces Henry Adams once identified as the Virgin and the Dynamo. I do not mean to suggest, of course, that Adams would equate Chartres with the old, pre-Podhoretz *Commentary*, or that American academics should be regarded as doppelgängers with the forty-foot dynamos Adams regarded as "a moral force, much as the early Christians felt the Cross." Nor do I mean to suggest analogies between Adams's equation of sex-as-strength and what Dylan Thomas means by the "force that through the green fuse drives the flower." Rather, I mean to point out two radically differing versions of power: power as it once applied to our best writers and power as it currently operates in the Academy. Johnson too quickly restricts power to a single force, one that fits his revisionist versions of our intellectual past and his giddy prescriptions for our neoconservative present. There is a power that also signifies the engagement of free, rather than ideologically grounded, minds, ranging over the cultural terrain and caring deeply about the moral consequences of their words.

That said, however, I would be quick to admit that romantic distortions have a part to play in my own version of belles lettres (how could they not?), but even if the generation of intellectuals I came to read in early adulthood were neither as wise nor as wonderful as I had once imagined, even if assessments of their impact and importance have been tempered by time, the shape and ring of their paragraphs endure. Nothing written in the tortured jargon of academic discourse says as much about linguistics as Orwell's single essay, "Politics and the English Language," and no study of the New York intellectuals tells us more about what the group's life was like and what it came to than this single paragraph from Irving Howe's *World of Our Fathers* (1976):

> In the sixties well-placed young professors and radical students would denounce the "success," sometimes the "sellout" of the New York Jewish intellectuals. Their attitude reminds one a little of George Orwell's remark about wartime France: Only a Petain could afford the luxury of asceticism, ordinary people had to live by the necessities of materialism. But really, when you come to think of it, what did this "success" of the intellectuals amount to? A decent or a good job, a chance to earn extra money by working hard, and in the case of a few, like Trilling and Kazin, some fame beyond New York – rewards most European intellectuals would take for granted, so paltry would they seem. For the New York writers who lived through the thirties expecting never to have a job at all, a regular pay check might be remarkable; but in the American

scale of things it was very modest indeed. . . . [Success] was simply one of the possibilities of adult life, a possibility, like failure, heavy with moral risks and disappointment. The whole business: debts, overwork, varicose veins, alimony, drinking, quarrels, hemorrhoids, depletion, the recognition that one might not prove to be another T. S. Eliot, but also some good things, some lessons learned, some "rags of time" salvaged and precious.

Like modernism itself, the New York intellectuals could triumph over everything except their own successes. America, especially its academic institutions, had the capacity to absorb dissent faster than those in what was known as the "adversary culture" could generate it. Academic life has been powerful enough, resilient enough, perhaps even savvy enough, to domesticate much wider ranges of knowledge than most literary intellectuals would have thought possible. What was something of a cottage industry for those whose essays first championed the cause of difficult, demanding modernist writers such as Kafka or Joyce, Eliot or Mann has become the stuff of symposia and specialized journals, Ph.D. dissertations and undergraduate courses.

Small wonder, then, that a generation of aging intellectuals seems to have *nearly* given in to the feeling that all the genuinely important work has already been done, and that most of what passes for the new — "The Semiotics of Rap Music," "Oppression-as-Housework" — is not worth the doing. To read Alfred Kazin on the "landscape" of American literature or Irving Howe on "characterization" in fiction is to detect, beneath the snap of their sentences and the continuing brilliance of their insights, a nagging sense that history itself may well end when they do. And if one has certain intellectuals in mind — that is, the people who write for a larger public about issues of public importance — these suspicions might well, might sadly, prove all too true.